Bibbulmun for the Broken-Hearted

Colin Valentine

Published by Colin Valentine, 2021.

While every precaution has been taken in the preparation of this book, the publisher assumes no responsibility for errors or omissions, or for damages resulting from the use of the information contained herein.

BIBBULMUN FOR THE BROKEN-HEARTED

First edition. March 7, 2021.

Copyright © 2021 Colin Valentine.

ISBN: 979-8224842339

Written by Colin Valentine.

Table of Contents

Introduction

This is not a guide book to the Bibbulmun Track. It's not a guide to anything really. There are plenty of guide books out there if that's what you're looking for and the internet is full of advice from many who know what they are talking about and some who don't, all of whom are more than happy to tell you how you should or shouldn't do things. I have no desire to be one of those people.

This little book is simply an account of a relationship that went wrong and a walk that went right; of why I did the Bibbulmun and how I did it; my experiences, thoughts and impressions from along the way. It's about people and places and wildlife and walking. It's about life.

Some of this book, like the track itself, wanders, ambling off in different directions before once more getting back on route. On occasion I have tried to offer encouragement, especially for those who may be contemplating the Bibbulmun–or any other long distance walk for that matter–those who may be new and a little unsure, or not so new and worried they may be getting past it all. There is an awful lot of hype these days, bright colours and loud voices shouting from all directions, frequently overblowing one of the most natural acts any of us can indulge–that of walking. I've tried to simplify the act, bring it back down to all it basically is, the process of putting one foot in front of the other. These offers of encouragement are just that, nothing more. You're not obliged to pay attention to any of them. They may help put a different perspective on things but at end of day you should walk your own walk.

There are times I've been critical of places and individuals. These are purely my personal views and reflect in no way the views of other walkers or the Bibbulmun Foundation and those associated.

There are also times I make mention of people or particular places. For reasons of privacy and to protect the innocent and not so innocent, I may have changed or altered some of these.

This book is also written for those who have already walked the Bibbulmun. It's written for anyone and everyone. It's a story, nothing more, a story that wanders sometimes.

I hope you enjoy wandering with me.

CV
My sister's dining table,
Eastern Cape, ZA.
November 2020

Close Encounters of the Best Kind

The path I followed weaved its way steeply uphill through dappled shade and thick vegetation. Though not yet mid morning the day was already hot and my T-shirt clung wetly to my back. Let's just say I was sweating hard. My pack felt heavy and my breath laboured with exertion as I trudged ever upwards, hands dug deep in the pockets of my shorts, head bent with eyes searching for the next suitable spot to place a boot.

I glanced up, hoping the crest of the hill I was climbing would be closer than it had been the last time I looked. My body froze mid stride and I slowly lowered my foot to rest beside the other, all forward motion halted. Gliding slowly, casually down the path towards me came a snake, clearly still oblivious to my presence. It was beautiful, its long body a dull bronze, its head and neck polished gold, its eyes obsidian black, its tongue gently flickering as it tasted the air. For long moments I was mesmerised by its grace, by its beauty, fascinated by how its head and neck shone out from the rest of its body as though someone had held it by the tail and dipped the first fifth of its length in gold paint.

At five metres distance it came to a halt, suddenly aware it wasn't alone. Slowly I took a hand from my pocket and waved it gently in the air. The snake–a Dugite I'd decided–raised its head, expressionless eyes fixed on me now, tongue flickering fast as it tasted the air trying to scent me. It clearly wasn't too alarmed and though I'd expected it to turn and rapidly vanish into the bush the moment it detected my movement this didn't happen.

For a moment we simply watched one another then I took a slow and careful step backwards. The snake raised its head higher and froze, eyes fixed on me, tongue no longer flickering back and forth. I took another slow step backwards, not through fear or retreat but simply to make the snake aware of my presence, my size, and most importantly to show I was no threat. I halted and stood motionless once more, wondering how the snake would react, intrigued by this chance meeting and the unexpected behaviour being displayed.

The tongue flickered momentarily, the head lowered, gently touched the ground. I could sense the tension leaving it. The snake turned sideways then moved slowly into the vegetation at the far side of the path from where I stood, its body making barely a rustle in the leaves as it began to move down the hill towards me once again.

I remained stock still and watched with amazement as it glided past me at little more than two metres distance. It was clearly aware and cautious but didn't appear alarmed. I watched it go, turning around after it had passed and following it with my eyes. It glided back onto the path without increase of speed and continued on its journey, a journey I concluded it quite possibly did regularly, perhaps even every day.

Snakes are not territorial but do have 'home ranges', often following regular routes and paths whilst out hunting. As I watched the snake turned to its right and glided into the path side vegetation as though it knew where it was going, had done this all before. I was convinced I was on this snake's home ground, that I was the intruder.

I have met many snakes in the past but never before one that had given way to me but barely deviated from its intended route. There had been no threat, no aggression, no sign of fear. I felt I'd met a gentleman–or a true lady; a snake that recognised my presence on what it probably regarded as its path but had accommodated me politely and left us both to go our own ways with little delay.

I found myself beaming ear to ear, delighted by what I'd just experienced, heart beating a little faster perhaps but mind alight with the magic of that close encounter.

I was walking the Bibbulmun Track and though only ten days into a walk that would last another forty-eight I'd already asked myself many times just what the hell was I doing it for.

I was doing it for many reasons and this recent encounter, though not anticipated at the outset, in its own way justified the day, justified the whole walk. Moments like that made all the effort worthwhile.

A Brief Outline of the Bibbulmun Track

The Bibbulmun Track–generally just known as 'the Bib'–is a path of roughly one thousand kilometres travelling down through the southwest of Western Australia, from Kalamunda on the outskirts of Perth to Albany on the south coast, or vice versa. The area traversed is known as the Southwest Botanical Province, a region recognised as a major biodiversity hotspot, particularly for plants and amphibians. The traditional custodians are the Noongar people and the track itself has adopted the Waugal–snake or rainbow serpent recognised by Noongar people as the giver of life who maintains all fresh water sources–as the emblem used for markers throughout the length of the track.

Best times to walk are spring (September–November) and autumn (March–May) when the weather is clement and the days reasonably long. It can be walked during the winter months though these tend to be colder and frequently wet. Summer is to be avoided due to heat and bushfire risk. If you walk in the spring then it's probably nicest to travel north to south and in this way follow the weather. In the autumn the South to North option would be the best and for same reason.

The Bibbulmun is a very 'user friendly' walk with shelters available at roughly twenty kilometres intervals or every night. These shelters are generally three sided buildings with sleeping platforms or bunks built in. Each shelter has a rain water tank and a bush loo. The path itself, the shelters, water tanks and loos are provided free of charge, an unusual thing in this day and age and one to be applauded. Maintenance, etc., is carried out by generous hearted volunteers and hard working staff from the parks department. There aren't many tracks that can boast the same and I personally feel this is something users should be hugely appreciative of and grateful for.

The track in general is never too far from some sort of civilisation, be it only a major road. On a roughly weekly basis (other than during the first two weeks travelling north to south from Perth where there is nothing) the track passes through a town all of which offer some sort of accommodation, potential re-supply, and a post office for food parcels should you choose this option.

The majority of the walk is on well formed paths or gravel tracks through beautiful mixed forest, well marked and easy to follow providing you remain observant. The sections between Walpole and Albany are predominantly coastal and comprise a mix of scrub covered dunes and beach walking, again the paths being well marked.

A comfortable time for doing the track is roughly two months though many do it in half this time–or even less. The track can also be 'section hiked,' and some sections day walked. There are several commercial companies offering accommodation and drop off/pick up if you choose to do it this way.

The 'go to' web site for detailed information and planning assistance without confusion is the Bibbulmun Foundation web site.

So Why Walk?

When you undertake a walk like the Bibbulmun Track you have plenty of time to ponder and the question 'why do people walk?' was one frequently raised in my own head.

Years ago now I signed up with a professional overland tour company for a trip from London to Cape Town in South Africa. There would be twelve of us transported in a fully kitted out 4WD truck which from the brochure photos looked capable of climbing the side of a house. We would travel down through Europe, cross from Gibraltar into Morocco, head west through North Africa before turning south towards Mombassa in Kenya. After a two week break we'd continue to the southernmost tip of the continent, finishing in Cape Town. The trip would take six months and cost roughly GBP 2,000.

During a phone conversation with a very 'down to earth' mate I mentioned this planned trip. There was a long moments silence as he absorbed what I'd just told him.

"How long did you say it would take?" he asked.

"About six months," I replied.

"And cost? How much do you reckon total?" he asked.

"It's two grand for the trip plus any personal spending money," I replied.

Again there was a long moments silence.

"Eehh ... you daft bugger," he breathed, "you can fly direct from London to Cape Town for six hundred and forty quid and it only takes twelve hours."

It did occur to me as I ambled along forest paths that should this same friend know what I was doing now his reaction would again be slightly incredulous. No doubt he'd take pleasure informing me that for a mere AU$100 I could take a coach from Perth to Albany and reach destination in around seven hours. He would have a point as well. Long distance walking–or 'thru-hiking' as it's now commonly known–has only found mass popularity since mechanised transport became commonly available and the irony of this wasn't lost on me.

So why do people walk? When you ask yourself that question, when you look at the logic of it all–there isn't any. Why, in this day and age, should anyone feel the need to walk one thousand kilometres from point A to point B simply to get on board some kind of mechanised transport when they finally reach their destination and return to their start point. It's totally illogical. Or is it?

I suspect there are many reasons for taking a long walk, the primary one being to step outside the over mechanised, over industrialised and overly technical world most of us live in today. I suspect that deep down inside many of us yearn for some kind of simplicity, to get away from it all. Add to that the benefits to health and fitness in an increasingly aware world and walking becomes more attractive. But there is more to it than that, much more. Over the years I've done a lot of walking and from those others met along the way, the even fewer spoken with about reasons for walking, I've come to my own conclusions–be they wrong or right–about why people choose to undertake a long walk, in sections or otherwise.

The majority of those I met on the Bib, especially those attempting to complete the walk in the shortest possible time, clearly saw the whole thing as a challenge–and quite possibly a rite of passage. They were testing themselves–against both themselves and against others who had completed the walk in short time.

Long distance walks, no matter where they be, have for many become little more than a competition. These people generally have the youth, fitness, time and the money. Where the walk is located, the scenery it traverses, the language spoken, the cultures met and the wildlife seen all become secondary, nothing more than peripheries. The main aim is to complete the walk in the most time efficient way before moving on to the next one. Trophy hunting by any other name. I have nothing against this, each to their own. When you consider the plethora and popularity of 'extreme' sports indulged–most of these to compensate for the current lack of sabre toothed tigers threatening at the cave's mouth–then it's hardly surprising those of us not inclined to leap from buildings or attempt thousand metre rock faces sans ropes should look for something a little tamer, less risky, in order to find challenge, to feel alive, to be a part of something larger than ourselves and our everyday humdrum lives. Long distance walks or 'thru-hiking' fits the bill quite nicely.

I also suspect it allows a feeling of achievement, something that differentiates us from others, something we can wear like a badge of honour allowing us to stand out. Way back when we roamed the earth in small nomadic groups young people had to prove their worth by ability to hunt, find water, provide shelter, gather forbs and roots and berries, build fire. This was how our worth was judged. It may also have been a deciding factor in mate selection–I mean no one wants to end up with the local loser, do they. In this day and age with so many high achievers, everyone but everyone obtaining a university degree, how are we to stand out as a little different from the masses? By doing something unusual, by achieving at something less run of the mill. Amateur psychology I'll admit, but I suspect there is some truth in all this, hence the competition creeping in, the need to be seen to achieve more.

I was strangely pleased to see a number of older types enjoying–or otherwise–the Bib track. Generally they were couples, already retired, some early some not. Invariably the gear they wore and carried was relatively new and of the better, more expensive variety, this suggesting they were not life long walkers but may have returned to it after years of providing for and bringing up a family, or just recently chosen to indulge now they had the time and the means available. I applaud these people no matter what their history or experience. They were making good and sensible use of newly discovered free time, building experience, staying fit, creating memories to share in future years. It was always refreshing to meet them be they end to enders or the more commonly encountered section walkers. It's just good to see people out there making the best of it, enjoying it for whatever their personal reasons and regardless of age or perceived fitness.

Then there is all the equipment deemed necessary before such a walk can be undertaken, the feel good sensation from purchasing something new, the accumulation of stuff we as modern day consumers seem to thrive upon, the final wearing of all this new kit–a uniform as it were which states to all and sundry who and what we are and makes us recognisable to others of the same ilk. Suddenly we 'belong,' we are part of a group or gang or religion. We are no longer alone. It's fact, we seem to need to belong, to feel part of something greater than ourselves and to be recognised for doing so. Cyclists these days wrap themselves in clothing resembling dark shaded cling film and wear pointy hats and bug eyed glasses. Motorcyclists wear leather and tattoos and sometimes small dogs. Hikers adorn themselves in brightly coloured weather proofs, flash footwear and carry fancy packs. Movie stars frequently wear each other.

I also noted, with some, there is an almost fetishistic taint regards clothing and gear. Don't get me wrong, I'm not for a moment suggesting these people parade around the bedroom in gaudily coloured gore-tex rain suits in order to arouse one another sexually, or hump each other doggy style while wearing rucksacks and buffs–though they probably do both these things and several other's I'm not imaginative enough to envisage–but there is most definitely, with some at least, a touch of fetish about all this gear, almost as though the gear itself is the central point, more important than the walking, something to be savoured and drooled over, discussed in hushed, admiring terms in the corner of the shelter, other peoples belongings often gazed upon with eyes tinged green, or fondled and lovingly caressed with covetous fingers–little items of desire. I often wondered if this type of person went to bed at night with the latest outdoor equipment catalogue tucked safely beneath pillow, or perhaps trawled the internet for new gear reviews, a box of tissues close at hand.

Another frequent fascination is weight, pack weight being the most commonly discussed. At times I've heard weights of individual items–many items–being quoted in grams and there was no doubt an element of competition and pride crept into these discussions. I often wondered if those who suddenly discovered their very expensive titanium gas stove weighed 2 grams more than someone else's model lost sleep over it. I suspect some did. Weight is important, no doubt about that, but I don't think it's worth loosing sleep over and I don't think it's worth taking out a mortgage in order to save on a few grams. Rather discard what you don't truly need than spend a fortune on buying the lightest unit available and carrying it for weeks on end but seldom using it.

I have no idea what my own pack weighed but did note it appeared to become heavier as the day passed even though I'd drunk water and eaten snacks from it. A law of inverted physics I guess.

Early on in the walk I met one lass who had walked the track south then turned around after only a couple of days in Albany and was now headed back to Perth–doing all of this in a pretty impressive time as well. She was clearly a weight fanatic, her already lightweight pack had all the tassels and excess pieces cut from it, not even a gossamer netting sleeve for water bottle remaining. Teasingly I asked her if she cut her toothbrush in half and quick as a flash she produced the item from a top pocket of her shirt. Sure enough, the handle was a fraction of its former glory. When I told her my own was powered by a AAA battery she just about died laughing. Each to their own I suppose.

As well as this seeming fascination with weight there is, among some, an almost mathematical approach to walking. Everything seems to take second place to the figures involved, the totals. How much packs or individual items weigh, how many calories eaten and burned, the number of steps taken, the metres of ascent and decent, time taken at rest halts and overall, the variations in temperatures both day and night, even heart rates. Again it's each to their own but to turn a beautiful walk into a series of digits seemed rather computerlike to me. Is this how you measure the walk–in numbers?

Almost needless to say those who appeared infatuated with statistics required the means to record and calculate them. To this end they carried what appeared–if only to me–an amazing amount of electronic wizardry and the life support systems to keep it functional. I mentioned earlier how I believe many people undertake long walks in the wilds simply to get away from today's technology and the demands it puts on us–the tyranny of watch, phone, computer, deadlines–and I'm confident that belief is true. But clearly, as things evolve and we become more familiar with and reliant upon technology, it too has found place in wilderness walks. I can accept and in ways understand this. I still find it a touch bizarre.

I was told by one guy that for the ultra-light modern walker 30% of pack weight is electronics. I struggle to accept this as true but on occasions, when I saw the amount of leads, gizmos, dongles, chargers, batteries and solar panels being pulled from packs, I did at times find myself furtively checking the shelter's walls for a power outlet. I worry we now live in a world where technology grows and blossoms while the natural world fades and dies, our faculties so blinkered by the former we are unable to see the latter.

I carried a phone and E-reader. The phone I hardly used. The E-reader was a good companion and I read extensively, especially in the evenings. I'm as guilty as everyone else, to a degree.

An unusual type, fortunately seldom met, is the person who appears to consider being outside their familiar crowded and built up environment a challenge. They are tackling nature head on, as though it were a threat, a constant source of danger and adversity, an enemy to be vanquished. I struggle with that one, can't fathom it at all. I tend to see it as sad reflection on current society where some are so far removed from the natural environment that to enter it is to step outside their own comfort bubble and into an alien arena. In my head they suffer NDD–Nature Deficit Disorder. You can often tell these people by their inability to stop talking, the topic invariably snake bite, dehydration, spiders, storms or becoming lost. In the past I've met one or two who were genuinely nervous about it all and I wondered just what the hell they were doing there in the first place. I'd try to allay their fears, reassure them all was nowhere nearly as desperate or serious as they appeared to perceive. With some I realised my efforts were wasted, they wanted to believe things really were perilous out there and we were all hanging on by the skin of our teeth, each and every day filled with risk, a fight for survival. I concluded for these people to see things otherwise would be to lessen their endeavours and achievement if only in their own eyes–but probably more importantly in the eyes of those they recounted their tales to later. Maybe they had just watched too much TV.

I have also met a few people clearly doing a long walk with the sole intention of weight loss. Again I quietly applauded in my head. They were trying to better themselves, feel better about themselves, and doing so in a way that would improve fitness, provide life experience and possibly broaden their horizons, rather than simply going to a gym or relying on books and diets to attain their goal. I also feel that treating a walk purely as a means of weight loss needs to be done with caution. A lot of energy is burned through day after day of carrying a pack over large distances and in all conditions. Weight will be lost but walking should not be regarded as a 'quick fix'. To do this and remain healthy requires time–and a sensible diet. One guy I met on the Bib carried no stove and was existing on breakfast cereal and nut bars, not a sensible idea and I tended to worry about how he was doing. He dropped out before the mid way point though I'm not aware why.

The one kind of person not present on the Bib was exactly the kind of person I had initially expected to meet in plenty, perhaps due to me being familiar with European and American hikers. Dirtbags and hiker trash. Didn't meet a one of them–sadly. I'm not going as far as to say I'd put myself in that bracket but I do love the almost at times competitiveness to be daggier and trashier than the next person. It's counter culture at its very worst but still wonderful. I dote on it. It always brings a smile. Conformity to non-conformity.

Finally there is what I've come to term in my own head as the Rip Van Winkle's. I met few of them on the Bib. Generally you can tell them from long distance, you're suspicions confirmed as they get closer. Most of these folks are middle aged, mostly male, most walking solo. Often they look as though they'd been in the bush for the last few years, wandering around in a daze of sheer bliss and totally unconcerned by their situation, too absorbed in their surroundings to bother about anything else, simply enjoying being in nature and moving at a casual pace, tasting the country they pass through. Strangely enough almost all these people carry quite a lot of gear in generally large backpacks of faded, often holed canvas of primitive design. Their boots are invariably solid affairs, well worn and heavily scuffed brown leather. Sometimes when I met this type, took in their old fashioned but well used gear, their abused boots, their tanned and dust powdered skin, the faraway look in their eyes, I really did wonder if perhaps they had been lost in the bush for a few years. The nicest thing about this kind of person is the unmistakable pleasure they are taking in their walk. They aren't trying to prove anything, aren't trying to set new records, aren't concerned about the latest fashions or brightest colours or lightest gear, aren't doing the walk for any other reason than themselves and the pleasure derived from it. They look totally comfortable in their old gear, it fits them, fits their attitudes, their casual gait, the look of contented happiness on their faces. Those I met on the Bib were in the bush for no more than a long weekend or a week, simply there to get away from things, enjoy the peace and tranquility of the forest without any set plan or destination, no goal other than enjoying it all. One character carried—among other amazing things—a BBQ grill and enough steak for four nights, absolutely no concern for weight. He was there to enjoy himself and that included glowing coals and sizzling meat.

These were my favourite kind of people though on the occasions I did meet with one often few words were exchanged, neither of us wishing to interrupt our personal reveries, or impose on the other's.

So why did I walk the Bibbulmun Track? Good question. I believe that with me, just as with many others, I undertook the walk for a variety of different reasons, most of them personal.

I've always walked, hiked, tramped–whatever you want to call it, but I've done so on my own terms, at my chosen level. I've never ever considered walking as a challenge, an achievement, a competition. I have considered it fun, good exercise, and most importantly the best way to experience and see country. I've also considered it therapy. I feel better when I walk, both mentally and physically.

Walking is the best way, the only way, to experience a place, to be in touch with it, feel part of it. The only true way of knowing somewhere is to walk through it; to feel the sand or rock or soil beneath your feet; to smell the dust or water or rotting vegetation; to feel the wind or rain or sun beating down; to hear the bird song, the whistle of wind through rocks or its sigh through trees, the bark of a deer or the cry of a raptor; and to see the birds and animals, even if just fleetingly, or even just see their tracks and scats in the ground before you, where they've been feeding, browsing, feasting on carrion. I don't think you can truly see and feel country any other way than by on foot, at a gentle pace, your eyes lifted to what surrounds rather than focused on your feet, your senses alert, your faculties alive. To sit in a vehicle or train is simply to pass through, to be nothing more than a spectator. To walk is to be a participant. I like being the latter. Put it simply ... you can't do much window shopping from a speeding vehicle.

But those are just some of the reasons I chose to do the Bibbulmun Track. Another was a woman. Isn't there always one involved somewhere along the line? Or maybe I've just been lucky.

LC

A while back I ended up sitting around a campfire with a group of much younger people of both sexes, and one or two who weren't quite sure yet. We drank beer, we told stories, cracked jokes, asked questions, and we drank more beer. Kat, a teacher from the UK, finally asked all present to take turns and describe their ideal partner. It was fun though some expectations seemed a little high and left me wondering how much I might be lacking. I'd never really thought about it before tending to leave chemistry to take its course and send me all the messages rather than setting standards, having expectations and actively seeking. When it came to my turn I suggested my perfect partner would be me with tits. If nothing else this brought a laugh which is primarily what it was meant to do–but at the same time I had to admit to myself there was a strong element of truth in it. I led an unconventional life–though I prefer to term it 'authentic'–travelling regularly with no real home to speak of, my needs and possessions basic, even frugal. Trying to form any long term or deep relationship had proven all but impossible, most potential partners understandably desiring a bit more stability than I could offer. I'd become resigned to the fact I'd be single till the day I died and was relatively settled with this state of affairs, prepared to trade the emotional contentedness of a strong relationship for the independence I enjoyed. Then, only a few short months later I met LC–me with tits.

LC. Loose Cannon. According to the little dictionary on my lap top 'loose cannon' means *an unpredictable or uncontrolled person liable to cause unintentional damage*.

The term 'loose cannon' originates from the days of sail when wheeled cannons in naval vessels were lashed in place to prevent movement caused by recoil or heavy seas. Occasionally these restraining ropes would fail, the heavy cannon breaking free and careening around the deck as the ship rolled. The consequences for the ship, if not just for those on the cannon deck, could be catastrophic.

It sounds bad to describe someone you love as a loose cannon but it was a good and fairly accurate description. The term was never meant with malice, never used in anger or designed to offend. It was a term of affection, endearment, familiarity, even admiration. It's a nickname, nothing more. There were times I saw LC as a complete and utter disaster area, an accident looking for somewhere to happen. I loved her for this weirdness as much as I loved her for her conventions. Isn't that what it's all about? Acceptance, regardless?

I first met LC on a turtle nesting project in the far north of Western Australia. She was one of the main project's team leaders for that season's group of volunteers, there to monitor nesting rates over a long section of truly beautiful coastline. I had my own project to contend with and our only interaction was in the jointly shared office.

After a week of induction, training and assessment the main project began and that first morning LC managed to lose her hand held radio then bog the team's mini bus on a sand track she wasn't meant to drive down. Not the most auspicious of beginnings.

I was training a small group of local volunteers on a beach further north and had already given my own hand held radio to LC to replace her missing one. Half way through my session another volunteer came striding up the beach and relayed the happy news that LC had bogged the minibus. Two of my group had their own 4x4 close by and offered to go and assist while I continued with the training. At the end of our session we walked back to our vehicle and went to find out how things were going. The minibus had already been towed out backwards and LC now sat re-inflating the tyres before driving back onto the sealed road and setting off to collect her group of patiently waiting volunteers who had already completed their respective sections.

Strangely enough I was impressed. LC had coped well with a potentially disastrous first morning and seemed cool, calm and collected as she blew her tyres back up to correct pressures. She'd misplaced her hand held radio but had informed me and borrowed my own unit. When she'd bogged the van she'd dropped tyre pressures in an effort to get out. When that failed she had ensured a radio message was passed on to me requesting assistance, another message to volunteers informing them of the situation and advising there would be delay before they were picked up. She'd then monitored her own section of beach before returning to the minibus and extracting it with the help of a tow. What I couldn't understand was why she'd tried driving down the sand track in the first place. I asked.

"I've seen your Subaru parked at the end of it before!" she replied.

"My Subaru has a 4WD system, it's actually very capable in sand."

"Oh, I didn't know that."

And so it began.

Not only did I find LC attractive in many ways I also found her lifestyle comparable to my own, an unusual thing I'd discovered.

LC only ever worked in any particular post for a maximum of 3 months before setting off on some new adventure. For much of the year she lived out of her well equipped Land Cruiser, travelling where ever fancy took her, working only when she needed to.

My own lifestyle was similar though not quite so well equipped, my beaten up Subaru having limitations on space and carrying capacity, my pockets a lack of money.

We also shared similar interests; wildlife and conservation, hiking and climbing, snorkelling and swimming and paddling. As the weeks of the turtle project rolled along we spent more and more time in one another's company, indulging in our mutual enjoyment of just being outdoors in such a glorious environment.

By the time the annual turtle survey came to a close my own project had increased in work intensity. The mornings were becoming hotter and the hours required on the beach longer. LC came on board as my assistant and worked with me throughout the heat of late January, February, and into March when the project reached completion. That June she joined me in Africa for three months.

For the next five years that's more or less how we led our lives. We lived relatively frugal and very simple lifestyles and everywhere we went we hiked and swam and paddled and immersed ourselves in the country, its wildlife and wild places, occasionally its wild people. I truly began to believe I'd found my soulmate. I'd been single for quite some time before meeting LC, had come to believe it was highly unlikely I would ever meet anyone who understood, accepted and could fit in with my lifestyle and I with theirs. I'd become familiar with being totally independent and it took a long time for me to adjust. Sadly too long. On a trip to New Zealand I damaged an Achilles tendon and spent much of the remaining five weeks lying flat on my back, staring at the roof lining in the back of the station wagon we'd acquired for the trip. During this time, LC, with my encouragement and support, continued to hike. On one of these hikes she met someone she'd rather be with. After seven months of what I can only guess was confusion and angst she phoned me up and finally confessed this.

I'd anticipated it, felt it coming. I think anyone truly in love senses the changes instinctively, knows the relationship is deteriorating, is aware of altered behaviour and attitudes. I'm by no means perfect and was fully aware that in many ways I'd lacked, could have been better, could have contributed more to the relationship. Being merely human and a male too boot I did what most other's would do in this situation, I grasped at straws. I tried to make things better, tried even to alter my behaviour, become a different, a better person, someone LC may find more attractive, acceptable–all this to no avail. When love goes out the window it invariably succumbs to the laws of gravity.

When that fateful phone call finally came I still chose not to believe. I convinced myself it was all just some horrible mistake and that tomorrow things would return to normal, LC would still love me and we'd all live happily ever after. I refused to believe she no longer wanted me, it was inconceivable. It's staggering how so many of us, even when faced with undeniable evidence to the contrary, chose to believe only what we wish to believe.

Relationships are never easy and I often wonder if the increase in failures these days is due, at times, to unrealistic expectations combined with inability to see the bad times through. Relationships require work and commitment and both partners have to contribute. Somewhere along the line I must have been lacking in this respect all my life. The relationship I enjoyed with LC was not my first failure. Throughout all of my disastrous relationships there has been one common denominator. Me. Can't say it plainer than that.

You may well think that with a history of failed relationships like mine I'd now be so familiar with break-ups I'd shrug them off like water from a duck's back. I wish I could.

To say I was heartbroken would be an understatement. Only those of you reading this who have suffered similar loss in their lives can truly understand the feelings of devastation and utter hopelessness that ensue. It was as though the glass bowl of my very existence lay shattered on the floor and no matter if I gathered up the pieces and glued it all back together again the cracks would still be there. I could not comprehend the fact that never again would I laugh and joke on a long road trip with LC, spend the night in the back of a vehicle before a planned day's long hike, or climb Mt. Valentine in Tasmania on the 14th of February with her. It was as though my life had come to an abrupt halt with nothing ahead any longer, nothing to look forward too, the whole thing pointless. I felt totally without purpose, empty, my future a dark abyss.

I consider myself to be a pretty average bloke, not much more than an ego in a sack of skin. My sack was punctured and I deflated like a party balloon. I did what I generally do when my life falls to pieces around me. I told friends I was busy, switched off my phone, locked myself away from the world, curled up foetal-like in the corner and began to slide down that slippery emotional slope of remorse, guilt, anger, loss, jealousy, defeat, rage, despair–and worst of all self pity–and the deeper I sunk the more I consoled myself with alcohol and cigarettes. I can't suggest this therapy to anyone on the basis it doesn't work.

Amazingly enough, before I plummeted too deeply into the abyss, I realised this last mentioned fact myself. What a revelation. Practise makes perfect? Or was it familiarity breeds contempt?

Before you can begin to cure a problem you have to first acknowledge you have one.

One morning I awoke from the now familiar wine induced fitful sleep, head thumping, heart still breaking, both alcohol and cigarette hangovers at full song. I knew I wasn't doing myself any good, my behaviour beneficial to no one, especially me. I needed to find something that would occupy my time and my thoughts, something that would drain all energy so that when I put my head on the pillow each night I might actually find solace in sleep. I needed a focus, something that would–even if only temporarily–take my mind off current heartbreak, something that would absorb my time and attention, give me a goal. Most importantly I needed something that would force me to cut back on the excessive smoking and drinking I was now indulging. Grief, though treatable, can prove a fatal illness. I didn't want my bout of affliction to result in the latter.

I decided I'd go for a walk, a very long walk.

Phoenix Arising? Maybe Not

I was living in a mate's small cabin on the west coast of Scotland when I received that fateful phone call from LC in Australia telling me our relationship was over.

It was the end of a miserable summer and the weather matched my mood of despondency. Day after day the sky was a low ceiling of concrete, the sea loch through the window whipped into white capped turmoil, the mountains on the far side obscured by rain that marched across the water in sheets of grey.

That morning when I awoke and decided I had to get a grip and do something about myself I took a look around and realised just how fortunate I was. I had a roof over my head, a fire to warm me. I was protected from the elements if not from myself. What the hell was I complaining about? Jeez, I knew several people my own age who were already dead! The world was once more my oyster. I could do whatever I chose without having to worry about another's time, emotions, plans and commitments. I was once more a free agent, a leaf on the wind.

Digging myself out of my crumpled and grease stained sleeping bag, pushing away the mess of discarded half eaten pizza's, beer cans and empty wine bottles, I emerged blinking and peering and scowling back into the daylight, scratched my armpits and the two weeks of stubble on my chin and decided I needed a purpose in life once more, but what?

A long walk in the wilderness sprang first to mind. It may not replace the yawning gulf in my life made by LC's departure but it might just get me out of the rut I found myself now in, get me out before I got so deep into it I could no longer see out over the sides.

On hindsight I suspect this sudden burst of inspiration may have been prompted from memories of a book written by Doug Peacock, an American conservationist now recognised by many as a bit of an authority on Grizzly bears.

Doug Peacock served two tours as a Green Beret combat medic in Vietnam. I've read that during his second tour he was discovered trying to patch the body of a bomb victim–a little girl–back together again with duct tape. How do you ever come to terms with such an experience?

Doug dealt with his demons by taking to the wilds, spending summers in Yellowstone and winters in the warmer climes of the southwestern deserts. He had a GI pension, lived a frugal lifestyle, stayed in free forestry car parks and camp sites, lived out the back of his pick-up truck. During this period he hiked a lot, probably thousands of miles, and it was during these hikes he began to learn grizzly bear behaviour. He also learned how to cope with inner tortures. The book he wrote about this period, the book I'd read, was called 'Walking It Off'. I decided that's what I would do, or what I'd at least try to do. I'd walk my heart-break off.

I've enjoyed walking all my life. Walking, tramping, yomping, trekking, call it what you will. These days the popular term is 'hiking'. It's a nice word and I do like it but to me it sounds a little forced. When I imagine someone hiking somewhere I imagine them doing it with purpose, speed, determination. I'd class myself more of a saunterer, better still a stroller, a name that has been applied to me several times, generally by hikers. Much of my walking has been aimless and relaxed, long forays into the mountains, bush, desert or along cliff and beach with little purpose other than enjoying myself, enjoying the place I'm in and the landscapes; the topography, the geology, and most importantly the plants and birds and animals that dwell there. I've tended to spend a lot of time walking quietly and casually along game trails, no real direction or intended destination, simply there to see what I can see, what's going on. I've also spent a lot of time becoming lost, then un-lost.

Walking can be very therapeutic and even relaxing. Frequently I've found that not only do I thoroughly enjoy a good long walk I also feel much better, both mentally and physically, for it afterwards. I'm not a fanatical walker, not a competitive walker, probably not even a proficient walker–but none of this has ever detracted from the simple pleasures of walking.

So I would walk–but where?

The options these days are many and wonderful–or they were BC (before COVID). I've never been a big fan of the now highly publicised long distance super trails with famous names and umpteen books and articles written about them, tending to view them as congested conveyor belts of gaily attired and often competitive list tickers. I have nothing against these trails or those who choose to walk them. In fact I admire people for attempting and often succeeding in these personal challenges, I applaud their efforts, successful or otherwise. Even more I value their attempts because it keeps them away from the places I want to walk, feeling the more 'commercial' long distance walks are just not for me. One of the reasons I walk is to get away from crowds of people, not to immerse myself in the jargon, politics, personalities and competitiveness so often encountered on more popular paths, the clubby cult of it all.

I narrowed things down. I wanted to walk for a couple of months at least. I'm past carrying very heavy packs for long periods of time so the ability to travel light and restock frequently was desired. I wanted generally good weather. I wanted scenery and wildlife. I already had a motley collection of kit and a car in Australia. Yea, ok, I'll admit it. Australia is LC's home country. I'd be closer to her. Faint heart never won fair lady ... and I'm weak. I'd walk the Bibbulmun track and to hell with the fact it was a well known, respected and popular trail. Besides, I'd been thinking about doing it for a while.

So that was it, the Bibbulmun Track it was going to be. I'd walk off my despondency, my grief. I'd shed my itching skin like a snake–a Waugal, the track emblem–and emerge at the end a new person, reborn. Well, that was the plan and all plans require a beginning. This was mine.

I showered and shaved, pulled on clean jeans and t-shirt, socks, boots and jacket. In Kyle of Lochalsh I took my rancid clothing and sleeping bag to a laundrette and while they rotated tumbled and sploshed I shopped for fresh provisions.

Back at the cabin I cleaned the place up, disposed of the accumulated rubbish, put my long dead lap top on charge, emptied the fridge of sad and soggy salads, mouldy meat and contaminated cheese, cleaned it out and replenished it with my fresh purchases. I was feeling better already.

Cabin cleaned, clothing washed, fridge stocked with enough food, beer and wine to last a week, I lit the fire, put lap top, A4 pad and pencil on the table, sat down and typed into the search page 'Bibbulmun Track' ... and that's where it could have all gone wrong again.

The Internet. It's a Bastard

The internet is indeed a wonderful tool but these days I sometimes question if there is just too much information available for a simple minded soul like myself. Much of this information is conflicting which only adds to confusion; and much of it is false. But how do you separate the false from the accurate? Why, you spend hour upon wasted hour, chin in hand, elbow on table, eyes going square as you scroll through screeds of stuff generally providing you with detail you're not specifically seeking. Another problem is it's all too easy to find things you really would rather not know and by the end of an hour's session of internet trawling the wonderful idea you began with now seems like a potential nightmare and you're seriously having second thoughts about it all. I like the internet, it's a playground and a fountain of knowledge, but it can also be a maze and a minefield unless used with caution and a dash of common sense.

That night, back in my mate's cabin in Scotland, the first search page concerning the Bibbulmun Track appearing on my screen offered the usual host of personal blogs, trip accounts and forums discussing everything from quality of bush loos too how to treat snake bite. I dived in and began to read.

Unfortunately all this information can make the heart beat faster, not with excited anticipation but with trepidation, the venture suddenly appearing a dangerous challenge we are not prepared for, a daunting undertaking. In the first few minutes of using the internet I'd read of several people who had taken anywhere from a year to two and a half years in the planning alone, and a couple of others who had lost up to twenty kilograms in weight during the walk, one of them loosing fifteen kilograms in only two weeks. Immediately I felt intimidated. My own decision to do the track was very spur of the moment, brought about more by emotional desperation than ambition. At best I had four weeks to prepare and that included selling my car in Scotland, obtaining an Australian visa, organising flights and finding somewhere to stay. As far as weight loss during the walk was concerned if I lost fifteen kilograms I'd be loosing a quarter of my body weight which was not only out of the question but would leave little option afterwards other than becoming a poster model for malnutrition.

On and on and on it went. Snakes, storms, bad water, getting lost, mosquitoes, blisters, spiders, exhaustion. By the end of an hour on the internet I was amazed anyone actually began the walk let alone finished it.

Fortunately, once more, common sense prevailed. I surmised that anyone who could lose up to twenty kilograms on the track must have begun it carrying considerably more weight than myself. I also recognised that it is human nature to overplay or dramatise this kind of venture, to do otherwise would lessen the teller's achievement and potentially their self esteem and social standing. People like to blow their own horns, some at louder volume than anyone else, and none of us like to see ourselves as plain old ordinary, many like to consider themselves extraordinary.

I closed all those scare mongering tabs and opened one for the Australian Government. I began the process of applying for a new visa. I was still going to do the walk –Australian Government allowing–but I was going to do it my way–one small step at a time.

Half an hour later I closed my lap top, closed the curtains against the falling darkness, opened a beer and lit a cigarette. I had a think–another thing I'm not renowned for being brilliant at.

I'd walked before, walked a lot. What's more I'd undertaken considerably more demanding and less accommodating walks than I suspected the Bibbulmun would prove to be. I already had some little experience of the track having enjoyed a couple of overnight hikes to one of the huts and back with LC when she worked in Busselton, an easy drive to some of the lower sections. Those happy weekend outings gave me a reasonable idea of what to expect. I had the equipment, or most of it, and I knew from previous experience what worked for me and what didn't. On the A4 pad I began to make a list of things to do in order to undertake the walk, beginning with applying for a new visa in September and finishing with the walk's end in Albany sometime close to Christmas. The whole project began to take shape, began to look a little bit simpler, and I do like simplicity. Most importantly, by the time I'd completed the list, I had a positive idea of what I didn't know and what I needed to know. Now when I went onto the internet to seek information my search would be more specific, if nothing else.

I fired up my lap top once more but this time I went direct to the Bibbulmun Track Foundation website and stayed there. Deep joy. Sanity at last, everything you could ever need to know about the track and if there was something you couldn't find then you could contact the foundation direct and they would answer your question. If there is only one piece of sound advice I can offer to anyone interested in doing the Bib track then it's to use the foundation website and only the foundation website as a source of information and advice. It does what it says on the can. No fanfare, no embellishment, no needless expansions, no negativity and no blowing their own horn.

Late that same night I finally sat back, put the four sheets of A4 paper I'd covered with notes into a tidy pile, knocked back the last of my wine. In little over four hours I'd drawn up a complete list of all required to undertake the Bib track, everything from A to Z including a very loose day to day itinerary of the walk itself. All this was gleaned from the foundation website. I now had a clear picture of what was to be done, what was required, what I might expect. For the first time in several weeks I actually felt hungry and though late I poured another wine and sipped at a glass while I sliced and fried potatoes, tomatoes and bacon. My celebratory meal. I was getting a handle on life once more.

It's Only as Hard as You Make It

Ok, so you're interested in doing the Bib track. I'm guessing that's the primary reason you bought this book. Regardless of whether I'm right or wrong, thank you for making the purchase. I sincerely hope I can be of assistance–or if nothing else entertain.

I've said it before, I'll say it again. The Bib is a user friendly track. You will, I hope, enjoy it.

For a moment let's forget the planning, forget all the gear you think you'll need, forget the worry of forgetting some totally non-vital piece of equipment you may have overlooked. Forget about the weather, about calorie intake, about blisters and first aid kits and all the rest of it.

Above all those things the greatest hurdle you will have to overcome before taking your first step on the walk is what goes on in your own head. Don't blow the whole thing out of proportion, don't out-psyche yourself. It's a walk–nothing more. Just as importantly you are doing it for fun, for pleasure–unless of course you're a self-flagellating masochist–are you? No, I doubt you are. If you were then you'd be reading something like 'Beat me in Bondage' rather than this little token.

So first, a few simple questions to ask yourself.

Current belief is that we as a species originated somewhere in southern Africa. From there we spread out and colonised almost the whole planet. How did we achieve this?

The American Indians didn't have access to horses until after the Spanish conquistadors left a few behind. How did those Indians get about before this?

What did Indigenous Australians, employed as stockmen, do when they left their boots and pants and shirts lying on the bunk house floor as though they'd just stepped out of them?

Getting the idea? Precisely. In all the above cases walking plays rather a major part. It's how we colonised the planet; how the American Indians travelled and hunted and traded; it's what Indigenous Australians went off to do when they'd had enough of colonial society, food and work ethics and wanted to return to the sanity of their own culture and people for a while. What's more all this was done without Vibram soled boots, freeze dried meals, gore-tex jackets or ultra light packs and walking poles.

Walking is one of the most natural things we can do. We've been doing it forever. Why should it suddenly be a problem? Just because it's you that's doing the Bib track doesn't suddenly make the track itself any more difficult or different, just in the same way there is not a greater likelihood of a plane crashing just because you are travelling in it.

Another example. Imagine for a moment a toddler taking his or her first steps. Imagine the excitement, the joy, the pleasure the child's parents take in this, even calling friends and family to announce the event with unmistakeable pride. Or is it pride? Could it possibly be relief? Could there be some deep seated genetic memory from our nomadic days coming to the fore? The child has taken its first teetering steps. It can walk. It's normal. The parents already know it has five fingers on each hand, five toes on each foot, two legs, arms, eyes and ears. They know it can pee, poop, drool and throw up. So far it's a pretty normal human being. But now, after those first faltering steps, they know it can do the most important thing any member of a nomadic group can do—walk. Soon it will no longer need to be carried on its mother's back. Soon it will walk the full day by itself. Soon after that it will be able to carry small items and soon after that it will be able to hunt or gather or search for water. This ability to walk means it will be independent while capable of contributing to the group.

These days we obtain driving licences.

So, you can walk. At the end of the day it's simply a matter of putting one foot in front of the other, albeit for quite a long time. What's to prevent you doing this for the duration of the Bib track? Nothing. Don't overrate the undertaking, don't underrate yourself.

The Bib track is simply a rather beautiful long and winding pathway travelling between Perth in the North and Albany in the South. It's highly unlikely it will suddenly become steeper, rougher or more arduous simply because it's your boots falling upon it.

However, we do need to put a few things into perspective.

I've noticed how many people, when planning a walk like the Bib, do more or less as I did. They sit and make lists of items required, things to be done, estimates of time and food requirements between restocks. They buy guide books, pore over maps, spend endless hours planning. Unfortunately, with some, this planning–the lists, the accumulation of necessary items, the organisation–takes priority, becomes the most important thing, central to the endeavour. It's as though if they have the organisation perfected then nothing can go wrong. Not so.

The planning is vital to a degree, it's also good fun, building anticipation, giving you something to look forward to. But planning is by no means the most important element. The most important element is you and your ability to walk. What's the point in going to all the effort and expense and time and stress of preparing for a walk if you are not physically capable of undertaking it? The most important item, the one that should be at the very top of the list before lists are ever written, is your physical capability and mental attitude. Can you actually do the walk? Yes you can, but a little practise may not go amiss if only to bolster your confidence and save you wasting time, effort and money long term.

I don't know who you are or what lifestyle you lead. If you are reading this then chances are you're a relative newcomer to long distance walking. You could be young and sleek and fit or you could be middle aged and growing wider with every year that passes. Only you can assess your own fitness and gauge your abilities, but if you have doubts then here are a few suggestions.

We've already ascertained you can walk, that it's the most natural thing in the world and no big deal. Now all you have to do is ensure you can put one foot in front of the other for a sustained period of time without suffering excessively or breaking down.

The Bib track, if done casually, entails around only twenty kilometres of walking each day. There is seldom more than five or six days walking without the opportunity to take a rest day. None of this is excessive. The biggest shock to your system—once you're happy strolling around twenty kilometres in a day—is carrying excess weight, your pack. To my way of thinking that's the make or break. Generally our bodies are familiar with carrying their own weight about. If you're not familiar with carrying extra weight around for most of the day best you get a little practise before even planning your walk. Get yourself fit enough to feel confident about undertaking the walk before putting pen to paper to make lists or booking time off work.

Start small and work upwards. Use the boots/shoes and socks you intend walking the track with; don't race but amble, enjoy your exercise/training, it's not a competition. Beach walks, road walks, walks through areas of local bush. Just walk, you'll be doing it for a long time on the track, best familiarise your body with it. Begin without any excess weight and when you can confidently walk for four or five or more hours at a sensible pace and not feel totally knackered at the end of it or the following day, then try taking a bit of weight along—your intended pack.

Progress to an overnight walk, the pack loaded with only enough to get you through the couple of days you'll be away. I'll bet that at the end of the first weekend you'll be seriously reassessing just what you need to take with you, looking to discard items and reduce weight. The benefits of doing these weekend walks are many. You not only familiarise your body with carrying weight, you very quickly learn how to reduce it by discarding all those things you thought you might need but in reality don't. You will also become familiar with the things you do carry and how best to pack them. All this will not only aid fitness but also confidence.

The bottom line is that for much of the walk you will only be on your feet for around half the day and then you can rest and recuperate. What's the big deal? If you are capable of doing this before you even begin to sit down and make lists and plans then you're already in with a good fighting chance. You've already eliminated the primary reason for most failures to complete the walk–you. More importantly you've removed your biggest concern. Can I do it? You now know you can. You are the single most important item you will carry on the track, everything else is secondary and will fall into place. Wearing the right coloured pants or carrying the most fuel efficient stove will not improve your chances of getting to the end of the track. It's a no brainer really. I've yet to hear of anyone failing to complete a long distance walk because their tent pegs bent or their Swiss Army knife became blunt. I've heard of plenty of people who've broken down or become exhausted.

Having said all that, having suggested a loose training regime, having advised you are confident about your own abilities before even contremplating all the other preparations necessary, I'll confess I didn't do anything like that. Nothing like it at all. The complete opposite in fact. But then again how many of us listen to our own advice?

That night back in my mate's cabin in Scotland I'd completed all I could think of at the time in four short hours. For sure there was still a lot to do but already I had a good mental picture of the walk and even a loose day to day itinerary scribbled down.

My visa for Australia came through shortly after and the moment it was confirmed I booked flights to Perth and a couple of nights in the Ocean Beach Hotel in Cottesloe.

I like Perth, it's one of the very few cities I don't mind being in. Perth has space, it has light, it has the biggest skies imaginable, and it has the ocean on its doorstep. Much of Perth has an almost 'country town' feel remaining, the people are easy going, friendly and generally upbeat. Smiling comes easily and naturally.

The Ocean Beach Hotel is an old haunt of mine. It's not top notch but has a nice 'used' feel to it. It sits only a minute's walk from the ocean, is reasonably priced, perfectly comfortable and has easy access to a few good eateries. Most importantly I've always found the staff welcoming, happy and more than helpful. Sod the cracks beneath the faded paintwork, the people are truly pleasant.

Like most establishments these days the OBH is non-smoking. I was given a room on the 3rd floor and for the couple of days I was there I indulged in a strict training regime which entailed eating a lot of Pringles and drinking a lot of beer. Every time I wanted a smoke I walked from my room, descended the three flights to the car park where I'd enjoy a cigarette before climbing back up those three flights of stairs and returning to my beer and Pringles. Perfect. After a couple of days of this interspersed with a daily swim and beach walk I reckoned I was fit enough for the track.

Between these arduous bouts of fitness training I completed the final details of my intended itinerary and purchased the few things I didn't already possess.

First Steps

The morning I left dawned bright, clear, sunny but cold. I knew because I'd barely slept that night. I'd hit a low and could only attribute this to the fact that setting off on the Bib track was going to take me further away from LC, if only in communication, something I'd foolishly allowed to continue since that fateful phone call when I was in Scotland. I also suspect my imminent departure on a very long walk without LC there to chivvy me on, share the highs and lows and all the little adventures, suddenly brought home the fact I had well and truly lost my best friend, someone I'd come to see as my life companion. Up until that morning I don't think I'd realised just how much LC's presence and company, laughter and smiles, had become such an integral part of my own life. It felt as though I'd lost a limb, wasn't complete any longer, could barely function fully without her. I was alone in life once again and found I wasn't relishing it.

I smoked a cigarette in the car park and had a think. I'd spent most of the last four weeks sorting things out in the UK, preparing for the walk, travelling to Australia, tying up the last few loose ends. During this time there had been regular and often lengthy contact with LC by text and phone call, in most cases initiated by her. At times it seemed as though nothing had happened, nothing had changed, and being weak I grasped at these little contacts, held them close like precious jewels, savoured them for days afterwards. But this situation only served to confuse. If she did still want me, something I was desperate to believe was true, then surely she would have said something by now?

At the time she was working in Nepal and wouldn't be back in Australia until close to Christmas. We'd planned to meet on her return and travel to Tasmania for three months. Since our break-up this trip had never been discussed, never been cancelled. LC had made no mention of the future and our mutual plans for it. Terrified of what the answer might be I'd been too cowardly to ask. The whole relationship still seemed to hang in the air, unresolved, and now I had two months to kill.

I stubbed my cigarette out, mind made up. Half an hour later I threw my pack into the back of the Subaru and left the hotel.

I'd arranged to leave my car with a generous mate in the north of Perth. He was at work by the time I got there so I took a last pee in his garden–it's good for the plants–changed into walking gear of shorts and T-shirt and phoned for a taxi. A taxi I hear you exclaim. Yes, a taxi from North Perth to Kalamunda in the south, more expensive than the coach from Albany back to Perth at the end of the walk, but I wanted to get going and half the day would have been lost had I taken buses and trains to reach Kalamunda. Besides, I like taxis, or more accurately I like talking to taxi drivers.

I've noted most of the taxi drivers in Perth come from overseas–some immigrants, some refugees. I'm always interested in their stories–where they come from, how long they've been in Australia, what they think of the place. Sometimes you get a story, sometimes you don't.

The worst I've found are some Eastern Europeans who tend to be dull and morose. They come from countries where the favourite colour appears to be grey and they haven't woken up to the fact they are now in Australia. Sometimes it angers me to hear such a person say they've been in Perth for 10 years and it's 'OK', this with an indifferent shrug of shoulders. I have been known to ask if Perth is only 'OK' then why not return to their home country? This usually heralds the end of conversation.

I'm biased. I like Australia–a lot. The place may now be–in many eyes–little more than a police state but I've always felt a freedom which is hard to find elsewhere. The country has a low crime rate, clean streets and a sparse population who are generally warm, friendly and upbeat.

More importantly from my perspective it still has wide open spaces; huge tracts of empty desert and bush and beach, oceans and reefs to die for, the biggest, bluest skies I've ever seen and an array of unique wildlife found nowhere else. What's not to like about the place? It is, to quote one old guy I spent a happy few hours drinking beer with, 'the last place'.

There are times I've felt angry, even deeply resentful, when I hear the country I could now no longer attain any permanent residence for being so easily dismissed, often criticised, by people I know come from much less fortunate and pleasant places.

Fortunately not all taxi drivers are like that. There are some wonderful exceptions. Strangely enough, from my limited experience, the stories I like to hear, the ones that warm my heart and reassure me there is still a lot of good in the world, come from coloured immigrants.

One of the most warming stories came from an elderly gent who originated from a war torn Afghanistan. He was in his sixties, clearly enjoyed his food, spoke excellent English. He was smartly dressed, his silver hair and beard neatly trimmed. Gold adorned his fingers, wrist and neck–his badges of success–possibly something to fall back on should the shit hit the fan in his life once more. Once bitten, twice shy.

He'd arrived at Perth airport over twenty years before with his wife and two young sons. Between them they had one cardboard suitcase and US$ 50. None of them spoke a word of English. They were taken to a small apartment where the fridge was stacked with more food than they'd seen in years. They were sure there had been some sort of mistake–this wasn't meant just for them, surely?

The following morning two men appeared at the door and my taxi driver thought to himself 'ah, so now it happens, now we are taken to the tented refugee camp with soup kitchens, pit toilets, sickness and disease'. But he was wrong. One of these men spoke Pashto–an official language of Afghanistan–and was there to translate. The family were to be taken shopping for suitable clothing and food they might be more familiar with, food more to their taste. They could barely believe it.

He and his wife took English lessons, learned trades, found jobs. His two boys were sent to school and received a good education. Now, twenty years later, he owned his own beachfront house, was semi-retired and worked only when he wanted, enjoyed being active.

I asked him about his sons.

"Pah!" he almost spat, distain and disappointment obvious.

They had been through school, both had obtained University degrees, they had apartments, cars, computers, cell phones and jobs–and still they complained, nothing was ever good enough for them. He wanted nothing more than to put them on a plane back to where they came from all those years ago so they could see and taste and smell and know what might have been–but they wouldn't go.

I could see the pride in his eyes, sense his feelings of belonging when he told me that even now, at his age, should Australia be threatened, go to war, he would gladly pick up a rifle to defend a place he valued so much. I knew he wasn't bullshitting, could sense the outrage and ferocity in him at the mere thought of freedom being threatened–and not just his freedom but the freedom of the country that had taken his family in and given them the greatest gift of all–a life. In return for that he was prepared to give his own.

I left his cab AU$50 poorer but immensely richer in feeling.

My taxi driver on the morning I set out on the Bib was Ethiopian, neat and tidy and ever so polite, and clearly not accustomed to his clients sitting in the front seat and showing interest in him. It's a long drive from north Perth to Kalamunda and after a while he began to relax. Sensing his shyness I didn't ask him many questions but did most of the talking myself, mostly about Africa and how much I enjoyed the place regardless of its many troubles.

Finally he warmed up enough to hesitantly ask why on this cold morning was I wearing only shorts and T-shirt, and why was I carrying boots with socks stuffed into them, my only baggage a backpack? I told him about the Bib track. He seemed amazed, had never even heard of it, his eyes widening as I filled him in with loose details.

"You will walk–in the bush–for 2 months! Where will you sleep? What will you eat? What about water? Why do you want to walk for 2 months?"

His questions were slow, quiet, posed from amazement and concern. I explained about the shelters every night, the water tanks alongside them, the towns passed through every few days where rest and restock would be available. He nodded in understanding, his concerns diminishing as he began to picture this walk in his head.

"You must take a lot of dates" he told me. "A man can walk a very long way on only dates and water."

He's right too but this suggestion instantly gave background and life experience. In a world of freeze dried foods, dehydrated noodles, energy bars, packet soups and hydralytes this man was suggesting a diet of dates and water. Though we sat close in the front of the car the gulf between us was vast, but here we were, conversing, exchanging ideas and expanding knowledge, offering advice. It felt good.

"And what about snakes?" he asked hesitantly as though almost afraid to raise the topic, perhaps worried it may be an aspect of the walk I'd failed to take into consideration. No one likes to be the bearer of bad news. "Are there a lot of snakes in the bush?"

I caught myself smiling, his concern so African where many are terrified of snakes and kill them on sight–not to eat, simply to kill. For a while we discussed snakes, me doing my best to reassure him that though there were many snakes in the bush the path was well defined and if I did meet any along the way chances are they would be as keen to avoid me as I was them. We were on common ground now, a topic he was familiar with and warmed to in the way so many African's do. There is little to beat a good horror story. He went into detail about a very bad snake they had in Ethiopia but never having been there myself it took a while of descriptions, habits and scary stories before I narrowed it down to an adder of some kind, most likely a puff adder, a snake with a justifiably bad reputation and found in much of Africa. I informed him Australia didn't have puff adders but I intended being very careful and treating any snake I did happen upon with the utmost respect. I would after all be encroaching in its environment, not it in mine. He seemed relieved as though genuinely concerned for my safety.

By this time we'd reached Kalamunda and the in-car GPS system didn't appear to have the vaguest idea where the Northern Terminus for the Bib track was. Neither did I, which amused us both. Here I was setting off on an eight week walk through the bush and I didn't even know where I was meant to begin.

He pulled over and with the engine still idling took out his smart phone. I noticed the face of it was shattered. Not wanting him to use his own credit or data I switched my own phone on, suddenly realising the act was pointless. Even if it did fire up in time I didn't have the foggiest idea of how to get onto maps or how to use them if I did manage to find them. The irony of the situation wasn't lost on me.

I was saved embarrassment. Before my phone was functional my taxi driver had brought up a map and located our destination. Leaning towards me and tipping the shattered face so I could see it he showed me where we were, where we had to go. I couldn't help but notice how the pale underside of his fingers contrasted with the almost matt black of the upper side, or how his hands looked as though they were familiar with hard physical labour. I wondered what he had done for a living in Ethiopia. Had he been a farmer? Had those hands held a hoe that tilled the dry and dusty earth? Perhaps those hands had scooped mud into square wooden boxes to be dried in the sun to make bricks for building? I didn't ask. It seemed too intrusive.

Five minutes later we parked outside Coles supermarket. He pointed out where the Northern Terminus was, just across the intersection. I thanked him, paid, picked up boots with their socks stuffed inside them. He climbed from the car, opened the boot, lifted my rucksack out for me, ever the gentleman. We shook hands and bowing slightly in traditional respect he wished me good luck and all safety on my journey.

I may not have had a mate to send me off from the start, didn't have family to bid me fond farewell, didn't have LC to accompany me for the next eight weeks of walking, but that Ethiopian taxi driver helped fill the hollow feeling inside me with his sincere concern and best thoughts.

I crossed the intersection to the official start of the track, plonked myself down on the bench, lit a cigarette, had a think. I knew I was procrastinating, delaying departure simply because it would lead me one more step away from LC, from the limited contacts we–or maybe just me–enjoyed by phone. Then I had a few words with myself.

So this was it … finally. At times like this, when you are about to set off on a long adventure like the Bib track, you should feel excited. The planning, the expense, the work involved in getting you to this point is behind you. Ahead you have all those weeks of walking stretching out like the endless days of a summer holiday when you're a kid at school. There should be excitement, anticipation mixed with a touch of trepidation, perhaps anxiety. There should be a quickening of the heart, an eagerness to get going, a delicious fluttering of butterflies in your stomach. Most of all there should be joy, your heart should be soaring. I was delighted to find I felt all these things and more.

I pulled on my socks, laced up my boots, tucked my sandals into the front of my pack and swung it onto my back, adjusting straps until it felt comfortable. A bright yellow and black Waugal beckoned, the first of many I'd follow over the next couple of months. I walked over to it, halted for a moment as though with indecision, then took the short steps down and into the bush. The walk had begun.

As a foot note to all this:

Before setting out on the walk, right from that first evening of planning back in Scotland, I'd made out a loose itinerary which suggested each hut I would stay at throughout the walk. I appreciated I'd probably not adhere to this, that in some places I'd walk slower, in some quicker; that rest days may be extended or not even taken. That didn't bother me, all I really wanted was a loose picture of how things might go, how long the walk was likely to take, my only target to be in Albany sometime around Christmas.

The wisest guy I met early on was doing as I was, walking north to south, but he was stopping at every hut and stuck to his plan religiously. Considering it's the first week out on the walk, everything is new, your body is adjusting and you don't want to overdo things, it makes sense to use all the huts if that's what makes you happy. They are relatively close together and the walking is easy allowing you to break yourself in gently which may prove dividends later on.

Almost needless to say I didn't adhere to my own advice, I did the complete opposite and attempted to emulate an olympic sprinter on my way down the track that first few days. Part of the reason was I couldn't see any point in ending my day's walk mid morning, the time I usually reached that night's intended hut. The other reason was without doubt LC. Earlier in the year we'd planned to meet up just before Christmas and travel to Tasmania together. We were still in touch—not a clever thing—and this plan had never been cancelled. I wanted to believe it was still going to happen and had probably convinced myself that come Christmas we'd be back together again, everything would be ok. Wishful thinking I think it's called. It was as though by racing down the path I was bringing Christmas closer, speeding things up. What bollocks. It was like wishing away time until a certain much anticipated date arrives. Notes made to myself in my journal read 'Christmas is when I hope to see LC again–but rushing down the track isn't going to make that happen any sooner. You're not trying to break any records–slow down, don't break yourself!'

After I'd picked up my food drop mid way to Dwellingup I began to listen to my own advice and take things a bit easier. It was only then I began to truly appreciate the walk.

Food Glorious Food

Other than a set of maps food was one of the few things I had to shop for in Perth. Food and gas for the first two weeks walking, half of this to be left just off track about six days into the first section.

Food should be a very important factor on any long walk, it is an important factor of any long walk. What's more, even if like me you're not a foody, then like me by the end of the first two weeks you probably will be. Food is fuel and you're going to need it, probably in greater quantities than you imagine.

When it comes to food there appears to be three main types of person. There are those who enjoy fine dining and are very particular about what they put in their mouths, generally preferring quality over quantity. Then there are those who aren't quite so fastidious but do enjoy that full feeling at the end of a meal. And finally come those who indulge both preferences. It really doesn't matter which of the above categories you fall into, so long as you are of reasonable fitness before you begin the walk.

I think a good rule of thumb would be that if you do tend to eat large quantities then you're going to have to carry large quantities. If you tend to eat lightly then on a walk like the Bib best you prepare to carry large quantities, chances are you will appreciate and need them. No matter who you are I suspect you will find your appetite and needs increase on a long walk. It stands to reason. Burn fuel and you need to replace it.

Though not a foody I do find our obsession with food fascinating. Food is a mainstay, as vital as the air we breathe and the water we drink. Without it we would die. Simple as that. Food, or the eating of it, has probably always been a social event. More recently it has turned into an art form, a profession, even into media entertainment.

Against that I've read that globally up to 25,000 people die each day due to starvation. That's a sobering fact. I write this roughly seven months into the COVID-19 pandemic and according to figures gleaned from the internet today's global deaths due to the virus totals 859. The highest rate recored to date was 8,513. Kind of puts things into perspective, doesn't it. For sure COVID-19 is a major threat to all of us, no denying that, but I do wonder if it's considered a major threat simply because it effects all of us and not just those unfortunate 25,000 others, because it effects you and me and not just 'them', those faceless masses.

Here's another couple of statistics that make me wonder, that contribute to me finding our use and considerations of food so fascinating. The internet suggests the current global 'weight management' (for that read weight loss and diet control) market was worth US$ 192 billion in 2019, and like ourselves it's growing in size. Against that is the figure of 800 million people who are starving in the world today–about 10% of the planet's population. Doesn't make sense, does it. Children starve to death while we watch Master Chef. Those less fortunate succumb to malnutrition while we ask 'does my bum look big in these?' and regardless of the answer dash off and buy either advice or chemicals to help us reduce weight.

I have thought about writing my own dietary advice book, but it would be a slim volume–no pun intended. It would consist of only one page, written upon which would be the words 'eat less than you burn'

Eat less than you burn. You won't find that a problem on the Bibbulmun track. I have no true idea about calories or burn rates or the rest of the jargon. I do know I started the walk at around 60 kgs body weight and finished at roughly the same. For sure I had to tighten the belt of my jeans a notch but there was nothing serious coming over me. After the initial two weeks of the walk I ate like a horse and could often have eaten more, fact is I could have eaten the horse with the jockey still mounted and then enjoyed the saddle, bridle and stirrups afterwards. I'd guess it's the same for most others.

Food is going to be one of the heaviest, if not the heaviest, items in your pack, the only saving grace being that it lightens as the days pass. The fact it is heavy doesn't mean you should skimp on it.

The Bib, as previously mentioned, is very user friendly. It's seldom you need to carry more than 5 days food before reaching a potential restock, usually a town with adequate amenities. I will add here that it's probably wise to always plan and carry one additional day's food for each section. Should you become lost (a difficult thing to do on the Bib but more of that anon) or should you become tired and choose to take a rest day at one of the overnight huts, or should the weather just turn plain miserable and encourage you to sit tight for twenty-four hours, then you have enough food to help you through that unexpected delay. Plan for the worst, hope for the best.

When it comes to restocks you have choice—aren't we the lucky ones. Some walkers make up food parcels and post them to either the town's post office or to their pre-booked accommodation. Some other's drive the full length of the walk dropping off previously prepared food parcels at pre-organised or planned spots before returning to their point of departure and setting out on the track. Apparently there are some who regularly meet a support vehicle, enjoy a full cooked meal and a short term restock at the same time. And then there are those who simply set off from their chosen start with enough food to carry them through to the first town where they restock as best they can before setting off on the next section.

Of those potentials I fell into the latter category. I didn't have the time, the inclination, or the money to post or drive food parcels all over the country. I probably don't possess the organisational skills required for such an endeavour. What's more I hadn't pre-booked any accommodation. Some of you may think that's all a bit slap happy, disorganised, even shambolic. I'll hold my hand up to all of those accusations. I am that person. I didn't deem any of it necessary. Sometimes I enjoy the uncertainty. Think of the time and expense and fuel used up placing food parcels, wasted to my mind, and for why? To give you peace of mind? To allow you to breath easy in the knowledge that food awaits you in each and every town at the end of each and every section? Do you really believe the people living in those towns survive on fresh air? Or perhaps you feel their dietary choices don't quite match your own? Other than in cases where an individual's dietary requirements are for specific health reasons I struggle to comprehend the need for food parcels. For sure there are a couple of places along the route where shopping is a touch 'third world' but there is still food available, you're not about to fade away and die. And where's the adventure in knowing everything is organised and guaranteed? Do we really need to know on day one what we'll be eating on day fifty-two? That takes a touch of the unknown out of it for me, removes some of the questions, becomes a little too well organised and mundane.

Finally, and most importantly to my way of thinking, if you pre-organise and buy all your food before departure then distribute it along the route, you are denying local outlets trade they would welcome and appreciate. Many of the small stores along the way do what they can to cater for walkers in the way of foods and gas, and all those I met went out of their way to be of assistance even if they didn't have exactly what I was looking for. Would it not be nice to put some money into their deserving coffers rather than into your local supermarket for a change?

So, now I've (hopefully) persuaded you there are options other than the fashionable food parcel, what are you going to eat? That's entirely up to you. Eat whatever you want and in whatever quantities you desire. It's your body and it's you doing the walk.

First choice with many walkers is freeze dried food which is nutritious, tends to be light in weight, and takes up little pack space. It's simple to prepare, requires the bare minimum of utensils, and leaves minimal rubbish to be carried onwards. It's good stuff, available from several manufacturers and offering reasonable variety. I've eaten loads of it myself over the years, but I wouldn't want to live on it. It also tends towards expensive, especially on a long walk.

I walked north to south, Perth to Albany, and I did make one food drop. The first section of this route takes the casual walker 12 days, and I am a casual walker. I didn't want to carry the amount of food required for that length of time though it is perfectly feasible. I bought a paint bucket with a sealing lid from a hardware store, stocked it with six days food, drove south from Perth until I was roughly half way along this first section then hid my food filled bucket in the bush quite close to the actual Bib track which rather conveniently gets close to the main highway south in a couple of places. For that first section I did have mainly freeze dried meals. This was primarily because they were easy to obtain in Perth and I hadn't taken the time or made the effort to work out a menu for this section. In the following sections I wouldn't have to think about what I was going to eat but simply make my choices from what was locally available. The other reason for using mainly freeze dried foods over the first twelve day section was to keep weight down. I may have walked a lot in my life but I'd spent the last month neck deep in an emotional morass, my only solace alcohol and cigarettes which I indulged with a vengeance, my only exercise involving ring pull's and corks. I was out of condition and after a miserable Scottish summer no longer familiar with the anticipated warm daytime temperatures of WA. I hadn't carried a heavy pack for months, had no real idea just how easy or difficult this section of the track would prove, and it was to be a twelve day stint without a rest day. Even the Romans who conquered much of Europe on foot and only in sandals marched five days and rested one. The Perth to Dwellingup section, comprising two hundred and ten kilometres, would be a bit of a baptism by fire. I wanted to give myself the best chance of success and felt confident that if I completed this section without a hitch then the rest would be relatively straightforward. I feel my cautious approach paid off.

For those who do rely heavily on freeze dried foods these were available at all but one of the information centres in each town passed through. The only item I myself bought on route was dehydrated scrambled eggs which I can highly recommend. I got four meals from the one large pack and this can be mixed with anything else you have available. It tastes remarkably like fresh scrambled eggs, an added bonus. Had I found more I would have bought it, the meals/weight ratio was good. Sadly it was a rarity.

For the rest of the walk I relied purely on what was available in the towns, on the generosity of others when I screwed up on one occasion and didn't have enough food with me, and on three occasions on packets of noodles left behind in huts.

I mentioned earlier that appetite will increase as the walk goes on. This was very true with me. The first week was fine and I lived on my usual sparse diet. The second week was harder but as told above I was very weight conscious initially. I didn't want to exhaust myself or aggravate a life long back problem. I wanted to complete the walk, not wreck myself. The third week I carried more and ate more and by the fourth week I felt confident enough to throw caution to the wind and carry what I felt was enough but never too much. With a body mass index like mine I knew I had to be conscious of intake, the last thing you want to do on an extended walk is start consuming muscle. Generally

I ate well and ate anything. Freeze dried meals comprised around 20% of intake over the trip. On one short section I had nothing more than porridge oats and a kilo of mixed nuts and dried fruit, while on the next short section I was eating pâté, fresh tomatoes, cheese and olives. I bought what was available and what my body demanded at the time. Chocolate seemed in demand much of the time. Snickers bars, peanut M&M's, Cherry Ripes (dark chocolate variety) were favourites. During rest halts in towns I'd pig out on brekky wraps, pies, fresh veg and fruit, steaks with salad and chips. In truth I'd say I almost doubled daily intake and often still felt hungry when I went to bed. I also drunk a huge amount of coffee and very little tea when generally the balance is 50/50. No idea why that should have been.

Mainstays were bread (usually in the form of wraps which keep and pack well and are convenient if, like me, you don't bother with plates, bowls, knives and forks), apples, peanut butter, Nutella, honey, packet soup; tins or sachets of tuna, chicken or salmon; ham, pate, tomatoes, capsicum, bananas, cheese, sweet biscuits, chocolate and coffee. Occasional's were freeze dried meals, salami, oats. Desperation was Deb powdered mashed potatoes with Oxo cubes and a few finger nails to follow. Snacks were dried fruit and nuts, often with a handful of peanut M&M's thrown into the mix. Delish!

Nutella was a funny one. I don't think I've ever eaten it before but in one place they didn't have peanut butter so I bought a jar and from then on in adopted the stuff. Spread thickly on a wrap for breakfast—with sliced banana when available—it not only went down deliciously but seemed to keep me going well into the morning. I'm still trying to wean myself from it.

Food can become a bit of an obsession and frequently, as I sauntered along, I'd find my mind wandering to what I was going to eat that night. These thoughts would turn to memories of wonderful meals enjoyed in the past, often into fantasies of what I might eat in the future, saliva spurting from beneath tongue as I imagined sinking my fangs into a beautifully tender and moist fillet steak. I've experienced this before on long walks, this fantasising and obsessing about food. I believe it's common among long distance walkers and quite rightly so. It's fuel, it's what keeps us going, keeps us alive–and we seldom seem to carry enough of it.

Though I may have fantasised about all those wonderful meals I also truly appreciated everything I had along with me, meagre though it was at times. When you feel that a wrap filled with cold ham and lukewarm hard boiled egg is the most delicious thing you've ever eaten you begin to realise just how spoiled you are, how lucky you've been.

Another factor to be considered with food is that it's often a social event and a major feature of the day. If your main meal is supper in the evening it will signify the end of the working day, time to relax and enjoy the fruits of your labour. For families especially it's a focal point of sociality, everyone gathering around the table, enjoying the food, discussing the day, planning the future together. For whoever has prepared the meal there is the reward of providing, of seeing everyone eating well, tucking in and enjoying their efforts.

I noticed this celebration, this elaborateness a lot, especially with couples met along the way. There were times I found myself watching them disparagingly. All the fuss and bother, all the equipment they'd dragged along with them to prepare and cook meals, all the washing up to be done afterwards. But this was their social time, a high point in the day. It marked the end of another day's mutual achievement. It was something they could both participate in, working together, looking after one another, then sitting to enjoy the meal in one another's company. In many ways it was quite touching. Sometimes I envied them their relaxed intimacy, the almost tangible pleasure they took in each other's enjoyment, the way they cared for one another. There were times my heart almost broke and my carefully concealed disparaging looks and thoughts would turn to those tinged with loss, regret and envy.

I'm also sure these same people looked at me with the same disparagement, at my meagre provisions, simple meals and almost total lack of equipment with which to prepare and cook. Each to their own.

Noodles, a bit of a mainstay with many walkers. Light to carry, easy to prepare. Strangely enough I never bought any though on three occasions I ate and enjoyed them. On all three occasions I found these noodles stashed in the log book box of the hut, clearly left there by previous inhabitants who considered them excess to requirement or had simply become bored with them and didn't want to carry them any further. I did feel a touch of guilt when I lifted one of these packs covetously from the box, already licking lips in eager anticipation but feeling like a thief at the same time. I consoled myself with the fact it's frowned upon to leave food, even in the sealed boxes provided in each hut, this only increasing the chance of encouraging rodents to move in. I was doing the hut and future occupants a favour, I was adhering to the rules .... I was also hungry.

Here's a recipe for noodles created through outstanding innovation ... and a complete lack of other ingredients.

Odious Instant Noodles:

Preparation time 5 mins. Serves one (but only just).

Ingredients:

1 x Instant Noodles. (discard flavour sachet, it's all chemicals and salt ... and besides, you might appreciate it stirred into hot water later on).

1 x Cup-a-soup ... whatever flavour you have.

1 x anything else you can find in your food bag that might add flavour or more importantly bulk the meal up and offer some decent protein. For instance beef jerky, sliced ham (mouldy or otherwise), tinned chicken or even tuna.

Boil noodles for recommended 2-3 minutes. (Being a connoisseur of haute cuisine I found the noodles to be al dente at 2 minutes 17 seconds when cooked in a 1 litre titanium kettle at medium gas in windless conditions. For additional protein leave kettle lid off in the hope a few flies fall into the mix.)

When noodles are ready drain the water into the previously prepared cup-a-soup in your coffee mug.

Add beef jerky, mouldy ham, chicken or tuna or whatever you may have available, stir thoroughly and allow the ingredients to suffuse perfectly by sitting for two minutes. With luck a few more flies may join the brew.

After two minutes pour mug of soup etc over the top of the noodles. Mix lightly.

Bon Appetit!

I did screw up at one point, embarking on a long section with nowhere near enough food to get me through. It wasn't a crisis and I don't for a moment believe I would have died out there, but it wouldn't have been the happiest of sections had not someone up there who I don't believe in smiled down upon me.

The Kindness of Strangers

I'll begin this chapter by pointing out some of what follows involves my one and only bad experience on the whole walk. One thousand kilometres, fifty-eight days total, many people met along the way and only one bad experience. I have little to complain about in reality.

I arrived in Northcliffe on a morning of lashing rain and gusting winds, became a bit directionally confused over the last couple of kilometres and cursed everyone from myself to whoever had allegedly placed markers on the track approaching town. Much of the blame lay with the usual suspect–me. I was cold and wet and not particularly enjoying this point in the walk, and there is a tendency to relax attention when you're sure you're about to walk into a town. Let's just say I wasn't a happy bear that particular morning.

I'd done the last four sections of the walk with only one rest day, this taken in Pemberton. Ahead lay what is considered to be the most remote section of the walk; Northcliffe to Walpole through the Pingerup Plains, 142 kilometres and for me roughly eight days. A long haul with little access to the outside world. With this in mind I'd planned a two night stay in Northcliffe allowing the chance to rest and recuperate, gorge myself in the local pub and cafe, and do a full restock before setting out for Walpole. Don't you just love it when plans go wrong.

When I finally did stumble into town, soaked from the waist down, boots squelching with every step, rucksack weighing heavily with water, I was not in the best frame of mind but at the same time was delighted to be there. Two days rest awaited, an opportunity to wash and dry sodden gear, take a shower, sleep in a warm bed, and most importantly there would be pies and steak and salad and beer and wine and more wine. I was already imagining the char grilled sirloin steak hot and aromatic and leaking its juices, nestled in a gathering of chips, a crisp green salad anointed with olive oil and balsamic alongside, a full glass of rich robust wine glinting ruby red in the atmospheric light of the warm pub. Bliss.

The information centre looked shiny, new, large and impressive, so new and impressive I rather self consciously dropped my sodden rucksack outside the door and removed my water filled and muddy boots before entering. The inside was just as impressive. Warm, well lit with expansive windows, spacious and airy. Sadly it was a case of never judge a book by its cover. I'm guessing the staff in these information centres work there on a voluntary basis, I'm not sure. If this is the case then they are to be applauded for their altruism, respected for their contribution to community. Those in the Northcliffe centre require training, I got the impression they weren't really quite sure what they were doing there, what their role was. If, on the other hand, these staff are fully trained and paid handsomely for their efforts, those in the Northcliffe centre require–hmm, how can I put this? Probably best I don't. Considering all the other Information Centres I visited even if just to log my arrival and departure date for walk statistics, the one in Northcliffe stood out like a sore thumb, and not for friendliness and efficiency. Enough said.

The lady behind the reception desk was kind enough to tear her attentions from the game of solitaire she was playing on the computer only long enough to point me in the direction of the Bibbulmun log book which I then duly signed and dated and gave a departure date for two days hence. The same lady, when asked about accommodation in the town, looked briefly up from her screen and pointed to the small selection of brochures laid out on the counter. When I said I was simply looking for somewhere cheap and cheerful she regarded me as though I were pond life. Fair do's, I probably did look as though I'd only recently emerged from some stagnant pool deep in the forest and possibly smelt like it too. I turned my attentions to the second member of staff who had been rearranging the postcards on a stand since I'd entered. On being asked the same question she shrugged and re-directed me to the reception desk. This may all be small potatoes, of little consequence, but to me at the time it stood out. Clearly it still does today. After years of spending considerable amount of time in Australia, a country I regard very highly, this was probably the most un-Australian moment I've ever experienced. Maybe I've just come to expect too much, but I don't think so. It was an Information Centre for god's sake, burgeoning with everything except information and distinctly lacking in a few other things like interest, manners and helpfulness. It was a very flash but very empty vessel. I voted with my feet. I left, my mood darker than before.

I walked to the one and only local hotel. The rain had begun again and when I finally found an open door–it was only mid morning so expecting a hotel to be open for trade was perhaps expecting too much–I felt guilty about the pool of water forming on the linoleum around my feet as I stood in the public bar and asked about a room for two nights. There followed a lot of tooing and froing between the woman I spoke with and someone who I guess was the owner/manager in a room down a corridor. Finally I was almost apologetically told a room would be $150/night but I couldn't check in yet, I should return at two in the afternoon. I voted with my feet again.

The cafe on the main street was almost empty but the atmosphere and the faces were warm and welcoming. I sat and enjoyed a huge and delicious breakfast of bacon, eggs, mushrooms, tomatoes and fried potatoes washed down with hot sweet coffee while the sodden clothing from my rucksack dried out before a gas heater the kind lady had moved close to my table for just this purpose. Suddenly I felt I was back in Australia again. My mood began to lift, but sadly not enough, the damage was done.

I sat drinking coffee and reading until mid day before stuffing everything–now dry–back into my pack and thanking the lady behind the counter hugely for her hospitality and excellent food. What a gem she was, what a nice place to wait out the storm.

The wind had dropped considerably, the sheets of driven rain now just a gentle drizzle, the skies beginning to open up and clear.

I made my way to the one and only store where the food choice was a bit third world but the reception and assistance very Australian. It was one of those almost embarrassing situations where people just can't seem to do enough for you, the lady behind the counter even phoning around in an attempt to get me a room in a local farm-stay. At times like these I feel humbled.

My re-stock list was now just a soggy mass of ink stained paper, but that's a lame excuse for my own failings. I bought what I thought I required, what I could remember. My head was still up my ass, my nose still out of joint.

My experiences that morning had soured my views and I opted to bypass Northcliffe and just continue on the track. It was early afternoon and Gardner, the first hut in the next section, was only fifteen kilometres distant. I could be there before dark, no worries. And besides, why spent around AU$400–a sum I could barely afford–in a place I no longer felt comfortable?

Strangely enough I got a bit confused on my exit of the town, just in the way I had on my entry. Maybe it was just me and my mood, maybe it was Northcliffe. Enough to say the place isn't high on my list of return visits.

Once I was back on the right track my mood began to lift. The sun was out, my clothing was dry again, I'd restocked and enjoyed a good if lengthy breakfast, even my boots had dried. I was walking once more, leaving worries behind. Soon I would enter remote country where I'd see wildlife, hear bird song. What was I complaining about? And then I began to think about my restock, I mean really think about my restock.

Long story short, after about eight kilometres of walking I'd worked out I was quite seriously short on food, had barely enough gas, and worst of all had only eleven cigarettes to last me for the next eight days. It could have been disaster. It wasn't, it was just part of the walk and any discomforts were of my own making. I had only myself to blame. I had no desire to turn around and go back to Northcliffe. I'd just tough it out, none of it was life threatening. These were my views until I reached Gardner camp. Then things did appear life threatening.

I like my space. In truth I'm probably a pretty antisocial and introverted bastard at the best of times. Throughout the walk I considered myself hugely fortunate to have shared the night's hut with others only 50% of the time. Often I'd arrive at a hut early afternoon, the place empty. I'd take a corner, sort my gear out, brew some coffee, dig out something to read or do some writing, and all the while I'd be hoping on hope that no others appeared and disturbed my solitude. If someone did appear I'd greet them sociably enough but underneath I'd be selfishly resenting the intrusion. Most of those I shared a hut with were perfectly decent, unselfish and accommodating–easy people to get on with–but I'm sure some of them felt the same way about my presence as I did about theirs.

I knew I was getting close to Gardner hut before I could see it. I could hear it. The noise reminded me somewhat of a turkey farm, raucous and incessant gobbling. For a while I couldn't fathom the noise, then I rounded the corner and the hut came into sight, a myriad of brightly coloured backpacks littered haphazardly around the outer walls. It was a school group. Deep joy–Not.

It was getting late, I'd walked over thirty kilometres already that day. The prospect of another 17 kilometres in darkness to Lake Maringup hut was an even less appealing option than spending the night in a turkey farm. I entered the hut to find it full of teenage boys, all seemingly competing with one another in volume. After a moment someone noticed my arrival, then another, then another. Quietness fell, so did the faces. It materialised that those wonderful people who manage the Bibbulmun track have absolutely no objections to school groups making use of the huts–providing they vacate the premises should a track walker appear. How wonderful. How considerate. How sensible. How beneficial for me and frustrating for them. I almost did a little jig when this fact was explained to me–and very pointedly reminded to the boys–by Mick, the professional guide leading the group.

Within minutes the place had been tidied and vacated, the boys now busy erecting tents and tarps and sorting themselves out for cooking and sleeping outside the hut. In truth I felt a little selfish. There was me with the whole hut to myself while fourteen boys, a teacher and Mick all had to cook and sleep outside. Mick assured me not to worry, saying it was good for the boys and they were all fully aware and accepting of the situation before they'd begun the walk. They had all the kit, they would be fine.

Both Mick and Chantelle–the teacher looking after the group–were nice people, the kind I immediately take to just on gut feeling. Chantelle, after initial introductions and apologies for intruding on my peace and tranquility, pretty much kept herself to herself, but Mick and I sat and chatted. Mick was a cross between a modern day outdoor instructor and one of those 70's types who had long hair, wore headbands and said 'peace man' a lot. I'll confess I was one of them once upon a time, one of those filthy degenerate hippy types. It was bliss. Oh come on, don't we all have some moments from our past we enjoyed but that can still make us cringe a little to remember?

Naturally–considering how and where we met–Mick and I shared similar interests and pastimes. It also materialised we shared the same mate, Nick, a good friend from Tasmania who had actually been Mick's assessor when he qualified as an outdoor instructor. Common ground. Small villages. Sometimes the world can seem a tiny place.

I was starving and as we chatted I began emptying my food bag, wondering what I could eat that would require minimum gas while still leaving enough food and fuel for the following seven days. Mick commented on my rather meagre supplies, pointing out there was no town for at least a week. I confessed my ineptitude without shame. The fault was entirely mine and I was confident that though the next few days wouldn't be the most comfortable I'd be fine. We exchanged a few stories on other balls ups and epics we'd experienced before he moved off and left me to my meal.

The following morning I was up and gone well before the school group, fully aware they would join me in camp once more that evening but wanting to walk the day by myself. If I recall correctly this was the first day of march fly murder, a fact that only hastened me along the track. I only ever walked in shorts, this delighting these winged velociraptors.

At that night's camp another while was spent chatting with Mick who casually informed me his group—only one of several utilising the track that week—were now five days into a ten day hike and the following day would meet a vehicle for a pre-arranged restock. I didn't think much of this until the following morning when Mick gathered everyone together and did a whip round before I departed camp, explaining to the boys I was a dipstick and was short on supplies, could they offer anything?

I left camp, my backpack heavier for three bread wraps, a 200gm foil sachet of salmon, and a double serving of freeze dried vegetarian stir fry. This was enough for two main meals and a breakfast. I was hugely appreciative and quite touched by the consideration and generosity shown. For sure the group were due a restock at midday but they were teenagers for god's sake, if they weren't fed every two hours they'd probably start eating each other.

To Mick the guide, Chantelle the teacher, and to all fourteen boys–should any of you read this my heartfelt thanks. You bolstered my supplies. More importantly you bolstered my often flagging faith in human nature. You are kind, considerate and generous people. Please don't change. The world needs more like you.

I began this chapter with a tale of experiences in Northcliffe, recounting things as accurately as memory and notes allow. Those experiences are mine and mine alone, recounted from only my perspective and are not a reflection on experiences other's may have had in the same place, or a reflection on Information Centres in general–quite the contrary in fact.

When you walk the track you are expected to log in your arrival/departure at every hut and at the Information Centres in each town. This allows the organisers to verify your progress if and when you register completing the walk. More importantly, should you disappear somewhere in the boondocks, it allows the authorities to trace your movements.

The Information Centres themselves, in many cases though not all, stock freeze dried meals, gas, Bibbulmun Track maps, items of outdoor clothing. In some I saw camping utensils and even walking poles. The staff can also inform you of track conditions, deviations, fire risk and weather should you not be able to access this information yourself. Generally the Information Centres provide an efficient and welcome service, the staff often going out of their way to be of assistance.

When I arrived in Dwellingup, the first town reached if you do the track north to south, my first stop was the Information Centre.

I'd found a pair of very expensive looking prescription reading glasses lying in their protective case on the track. I wanted to hand these in ASAP in case someone was desperately looking for them. I also needed some sort of accommodation organised. I was on a tight budget and happily settled for a walkers room in the caravan park. The considerate girl at reception not only phoned to confirm a room was available, she also booked me in–and then offered to drive me up there, explaining it was at least a kilometre out of town and would be hard work with the backpack I was carrying. I was touched and amused. How sweet and considerate. I thanked her genuinely but declined the offer.

Exactly the same thing happened in Pemberton. The lady at reception not only booked me into the motel but then offered to drive me up there, explaining it was quite a walk and mostly uphill. She was right. Again I was touched by the consideration shown but declined her offer.

In the tiny Information Centre in Ballingup, after signing the log book, I explained to the lady at reception I was only intending to spend one night in town, leaving early the following morning, no rest halt. I also pointed out I was strapped for cash and wondered if it would be ok if I slept down at the football field's amenities where I'd be under cover should it rain. This wasn't a problem at all, I was more than welcome to spend the night there. Should I wish to use the showers in the changing rooms it would cost $7, expensive for a shower but cheap as chips for a night. I paid happily. I also needed gas but the Information Centre had run out and was awaiting fresh stock, the lady suggesting I try the small store at the fuel station. A couple of hours later I was sitting enjoying a sandwich and coffee at an outside table of the Pie Bakery when same lady walked past. She stopped and asked if I'd managed to obtain gas OK. Again I was touched by the consideration shown.

The toasted sandwich I was eating was a delicious mix of grilled bacon, egg, cheese and spinach. The lady who served me provided a small sealed tub of mayonnaise to be taken along on the next walk section, no charge.

The store adjoining the fuel station in Ballingup is by no means large but does stock most things you're likely to require. It's only three days walk to Donnelly River where again you'll find the basics. With it being such a short section I decided to splash out on fresh food and in the little store purchased–among other things–eggs, ham and fresh tomatoes–sod the weight. The guy behind the counter asked if I was doing the track and when I confirmed this he asked when I intended leaving. I told him around six the following morning. He then informed me the fuel station opened before then and if I liked I could leave my fresh food purchases with him and he'd put them in cold storage for the night, I could collect them on my way out of town. So thoughtful. I took him up on his kind offer.

Probably one of the most appreciated gestures came from Sue who works at Donnelly River. I was only there for one night and after checking in, taking a shower and washing my clothing at the same time, I wandered down to the tiny store for a restock. The place is small but they do their best to cater for walkers and as it's only five days walk to the town of Pemberton you're unlikely to die of malnutrition before getting there. The store didn't sell cigarettes but no worries, I had a few remaining. They didn't appear to sell beer or wine either which was a bit of a blow, I'd been looking forward to a cold one for the past three days, one of those little fantasies you indulge along the way. Being a bit brass necked I thought I'd ask. Sue explained they didn't have an alcohol licence so could not sell beer. She did however have a few cold ones in her fridge at home and she'd happily provide me with a couple but could not and would not accept any payment for them. My arm was twisted. God but that beer tasted good.

In the pub in Pemberton I met Dave, a guy who owned the local marron outlet. When I showed interest, explaining my ignorance of these and all the other varieties of fresh water crayfish found in WA, Dave invited me to spend some time at his premises. I accepted the offer gratefully and passed a happy couple of hours with him, drinking his coffee and learning more about marron. He was generous and good company, interesting and informative without over complicating things.

In his office stood a glass tank with live marron in it. These were blue marron, very rare, very unusual, very beautiful. They were there as display only, a feature of interest.

Mid way through the afternoon a car load of Chinese tourists appeared, all keen to buy fresh marron and also trout, another fish provided by Dave. I watched quietly while Dave entertained them, led them around the tanks, explained the contents and how best to cook them. The Chinese tourists made their own selection, pointing and gesticulating towards exactly the creature they desired while Dave fished them out and packaged them. One of these tourists had made his way independently through to the office where he'd laid eyes on the blue marron on display. He enquired about them. The more Dave tried to explain they were very rare, very expensive and for display not consumption, the more the Chinese tourists wanted to eat them, at any cost.

To all these people (excluding the Chinese tourists) and many others who showed unsought generosity along the way–thank you. People like you enrich the whole experience.

69

People Met Along the Way

People. Ok, I'm not a people's person. I tend to like my own company. In the past I've been called everything from reserved and introvert to arrogant, aloof and antisocial. Fair do's. I've never meant to be rude or standoffish. I do tend to be quiet. Some people tend to be overly sensitive or fail to allow for others.

From the above you will gather I like my own space. When I decided to do the Bibbulmun that was a minor consideration. I accepted there would be others on the track, that inevitably I'd share time and space with total strangers. That would all be part of the experience and in some ways I welcomed it, in other ways I didn't.

I like to walk solo. I like to absorb what's going on around me, to pass through with as little disturbance as possible, to be aware of surroundings, wildlife, even just signs of wildlife. I like to listen to the sigh of wind through trees, the creak of strained bough, the crunch of gravel beneath my boots, the joyous gurgle and tumbling of an athletic little stream, the happy chatter of birdsong and even the raucous cries of alarm or anger, the clatter of wings as flight is sought. I like to smell the leaf mould and vegetation, the scent of bush or flower or herb, the dampness after rain, the ozone of a high mountain pass.

You can't do any of these things while engrossed in often mindless conversation while looking at nothing else but your boots. That's not why I walk.

LC and I walked well together, or at least that's my opinion. She may choose to differ. LC was considerably younger and fitter than me. She walked at greater pace. Put simply, LC hiked, I walked. Frequently we'd do a full day's walk and the only time we truly talked or I switched off much of what was going on around me was when we stopped to rest, snack, eat, swim or camp for the night. Most of the time we walked separately. LC liked to be out in front, forging ahead at her–to me at least–relentless pace. Occasionally, before she disappeared around a corner or over a pass, she'd turn and give a little wave. I would wave back, smiling at our contact, touched by this small and distanced intimacy, at the way she was checking up on me, making sure I was still trudging along in my own little world, saying 'hello, I'm thinking of you' in her own little way. It worked for me.

The only times we didn't indulge this style was in Africa when we walked in areas of dangerous game. At these times I'd ask she walked behind me and for obvious reasons I'd insist on complete silence and walk at a very leisurely and cautious pace. I could feel the frustration emanating from her, sense her annoyance, imagine her eyes boring angrily into my back. Often, when I stopped to listen hard or check out the ground ahead with binoculars, she'd bump into me so closely was she following. I often thought that had LC been a horse she would have required barbed wire around her bridle's bit.

But back to people on the Bib.

I knew the track was popular, knew there were nightly huts which in general could sleep up to 12 people but were often so busy it was advised you take a tent along in case there was no room left available when you arrived. I knew the track was popular during spring and autumn and it was late spring I would be walking. None of this really bothered me. The walk would be as it was and people would play a major part of it. That's the strange thing about people, about mixing with them while on an endeavour such as the Bib. People can make or break the event. People, whether I like it or not, play a major part in any event.

I've been hugely fortunate in life, enjoyed a lot of travel and many adventures. No matter where I've been or what I've been doing it's the people who have been the deciding catalyst on how you view the experience afterwards. The positive side is being with others who share your interests, enthusiasms and excitements, this only adding to your own enjoyment. They may well be unfazed by camping conditions, don't care if they can't shower for a week, willingly get mucked in with any task that has to be done. Quite often these people become life long friends even though you may never meet again. They have added positively to your experience, your memories. You like to believe it's reciprocated. You look back on the event fondly, as being a good and happy time, and this is in many ways is due to the people you shared it with. And then there's the other side of the coin.

For example: viewing elephants while on foot in Africa is a truly wonderful experience. But an elephant is an elephant and though you may derive excitement and pleasure from viewing it this can be enhanced by the tangible pleasures the people you are with emanate, or lessened by other's negativity. If those people are the type who talk too loudly and move the animal away prematurely, or complain about having to crouch behind a bush for so long, or become bored and want to move on before you have taken your fill, then this leaves a bitter taste in your mouth, the experience is marred, not nearly so rewarding as it could have, should have been.

Yup, people can make or break the experience which could well be why I prefer in general to avoid them and by doing so increase the odds of enjoying myself. And besides, lets be totally honest about this, perhaps by avoiding those 'others' its me who's doing them a favour.

That's the thing about people, you just never can tell.

Amazingly enough, more by luck than good management, I ended up walking the Bib during a quiet spell, a lull in numbers. For sure there were busy moments, especially at weekends or at huts with easy access from a road, but for most of the time I had little or no company. It really was just dumb luck. Often, when looking through the hut's log book, I'd note that had I been there only one week previously I'd have been sharing the space with twelve others ... and there was me, sitting happily on my own. The brief notes I made while on the track tell me I shared huts for only 50% of the time. Some of those I shared with I remember well, generally for positive reasons. I can only hope they feel the same about me–but you can never be sure, can you. On a couple of occasions I deliberately slowed my pace or even took a rest day simply to avoid catching someone travelling in front of me who left comments in the log books that suggested we would never be bosom buddies. Best to avoid the conflict for both our sakes. And inevitably there were those who though nice enough people did have some rather strange habits. Don't well all?

Tents erected inside huts. That one always confused me. Tents take up quite a lot of space–but having said that some people manage to take up a lot of space without a tent. Tents are often slow and noisy to erect and take down, this depending much on the operator. Tents have zips which make irritating noise in the middle of the night–providing you can hear them over the noise of my snoring. But come on, really, tents INSIDE huts!

There were times I could understand this ... well almost understand it. The case of women who wanted privacy while they got in and out of their sleeping bags. The cases of those seriously bothered by mosquitoes. Both understandable, to a degree. Why not just pitch the tent outside in the first place? Privacy will be increased; there may be a breeze keeping mozzies at bay.

The most intriguing was a woman who chose to erect her tent on the upper bunk beneath a pitched roof. It just wasn't going to happen.

Amazingly enough it did ... eventually. I don't think she found it the most convenient or comfortable of pitches.

As for individuals, people encountered along the way–again it's the unusual or the just plain nice, or not so nice, that spring first to mind.

A Frenchman, 70 years old, who walked with a huge back pack, a severe stoop and a very thick 2 metre long staff for a walking pole, a notch cut in it for each day he'd walked–I assumed. The first time I spotted him hobbling bent and crooked up the hill towards the hut I immediately thought of an exhausted pilgrim seeking salvation. He wore a full wet weather rain suit all the time, regardless of weather or temperature, having to lay it out over logs to dry the condensation soaked interior whenever he stopped. On his feet he wore Crocs. In my head and in deference to his nationality I called him 'Croque–Monsieur'. He didn't like people, didn't like talking, didn't like company. I could sympathise with that. He didn't like sleeping in the shelters, preferring to go past them and bivi in the bush by himself. On the one night we did share a shelter he opted to sleep on top of the picnic table out in the open, a 2 litre water bottle beneath the base of his back which was clearly playing up. There was an impressive hatch of flying ants, the insects filling the air outside the hut and in order to endure their numbers he had to completely envelope himself inside his sleeping bag. It can't have been pleasant, the night being warm. In the log books he signed his name upside down and wrote about the 'Creator' and the walk being through the 'garden of Eden'. I concluded–wrongly–he'd never been to Africa. Once I gave him gas for his stove, at another time I gave food even though I could barely afford to. On both occasions he didn't even know when the next town for restocking was due. He existed on a diet of packet soup and nut bars. Once, after he'd moved off the evening before to go and sleep in the bush by himself, the following morning I met him coming the wrong way up the path. I asked if he'd opted out and was returning to the last town. No, he was simply lost and had turned the wrong direction when he'd returned to the track after a night's sleep. It took a moment to convince him of his error until I pointed out the position of the sun which was still low in the sky. It suggested he was walking north rather than south. I worried about him, unnecessarily. He completed the sections of the walk he had undertaken.

A European girl who was averaging forty kilometres each day criticised my everything. The pack I carried which was far too heavy; the fact I'd hung my sleeping bag up to air and loft while I cooked dinner, a sensible thing to do but clearly one she hadn't thought of first so therefor it couldn't be right; the food I carried which on that relatively short section consisted primarily of eggs, ham, cheese and wraps none of which were nutritious (?) and all far too heavy. She actually asked–sorry–insisted on knowing why I was carrying eggs of all things. When I replied 'to eat?' she looked at me as though I were pond life. Having vented her distaste on my everything she demanded I leave my clothes line up as she wanted to dry her socks. She then returned her attention to the app on her phone so she could assess the metres of ascent and decent expected the following day, total the distance, work out how many steps she would take and calculate to the nearest minute the time required, this including four halts of exactly seventeen minutes. After that she turned her attentions to another app on her phone and having finally gone silent I assumed she was micro managing her after dinner farts. She made a jelly which would set overnight allowing her to eat it for breakfast. Then she ate half a pack of Scotch Finger biscuits ... her dinner. As she did so I made elaborate affair of laying out my wraps, spreading them with mayonnaise, draping them with smoked ham over which I scattered thin slices of Jarlsberg cheese before slicing freshly boiled and still steaming hot eggs over the top and giving them a sprinkling of black pepper. Deep delight, she drooled like a starving Labrador. She left in the pre-dawn darkness, just before the best birdsong began. Such joy.

At Donnelly River, while restocking as best I could from the tiny store, I asked if they sold beer. They didn't have a licence but the very kind lady serving me walked home to her cottage and took two cans of Great Northern Original from her fridge, refusing any payment for them. Against better judgement–not to mention personal need–I gave one of these to a young guy I'd shared huts with for a couple of nights. He was suffering knee problems and thinking of dropping out. I thought the unexpected beer might cheer him up. He didn't say thank you.

I would say the majority of those others I met doing the track end to end viewed the whole thing as a personal challenge and were out to do it in minimal time, carrying minimal gear. Many succeeded, others dropped out around half way due to either injury or from simply having hit a wall and having no energy left to continue. I can only guess that a combination of hard pace and minimal food in an effort to keep pack weight down resulted in their retirement.

The saddest I know of these tales involved a South African guy. He was built like a racing snake and carried the smallest pack I saw on the trip, probably little more than 30 litres. He was consistently double, sometimes triple hutting, averaging 40 kilometres each day, hoping to complete the track in well under a month. On the night we shared a shelter his sleeping bag was so light weight I could hear his teeth chattering even over the sound of the BeeGees coming from his phone ear pieces ... and this till the early hours so he clearly wasn't sleeping much either. The BeeGee's for gods sake, but each to their own. I later heard that four days from the end in Albany he suffered a foot injury and had to drop out. What a bugger for him.

I think my biggest disappointments came during those times I read negative comments in the hut log book. These weren't frequent, but they did pop up and sometimes I wondered about the entitlement some people appear to feel these days.

The Bib track is free, no charge to walk it. How does that work? It works because of the good grace of the Noongar people, the traditional custodians; because of the hard work done by the Bibbulmun foundation and the generous sponsorship raised; because of big hearted volunteers who give freely of their time and efforts to maintain the track and the huts; and it works because of government departments who keep the track open, maintain bush loos, clean huts, remove discarded rubbish and ensure water tanks are full and operational. All this for free, yet still people complain? I really did struggle to get my head around that one, what's more I failed. What do some people expect? Too much it would appear.

Undoubtably some of these complaints were well intentioned, written more to bring attention to a problem rather than just complain about it. I can understand that, those people simply trying to help. Other comments were outright complaints, in the odd case unnecessarily harsh. I can only hope the volunteers who do a good job of maintaining track and huts don't read them. I can only hope the princes and princesses who chose to leave these comments finally manage to get a life.

On the upside, one of the most amusing comments I've ever read was in an end of walk log book on a long trail in New Zealand. I can't remember it exactly but the writer wrote lyrically, extolling the beauty of the walk, the outstanding scenery, river and ridge crossings. Most of all he praised the remoteness, the isolation, the complete lack of human presence and impact. It was, in his opinion, the wildest most untouched and natural place on earth and this is what made it so special–but could we have a few more path signs please.

Occasionally in the hut log books I'd read complaints about others sharing the hut, especially in those huts easily accessible by vehicle. These complaints would refer to local families taking over the hut at weekends, lighting fires, drinking till all hours and generally having a good time, their noise and behaviour offending those walking the track and requiring sleep–not to mention fair space in the hut. For sure it happens, people are people, some considerate, some not.

I approached Grimwade hut in the middle of a hot, sultry and thunder threatening afternoon. The day had only been twenty-three kilometres but between topography and humidity it had been a hard one. As I approached the hut I heard voices and hopes of a nice quite time by myself faded. No worries. And then I saw vehicles, several of them, all 4x4's parked haphazardly around the place. I spotted tents scattered amongst the bush behind the hut. Even more depressing was the sight of a gaily coloured gazebo erected right outside the hut where the picnic table usually stood. My heart fell. It was a Saturday, there were a heap of utes parked at the hut, tents surrounding it, shade erected outside it. Whoever these people were they were here for a while and had taken the place over. I immediately suspected it would be locals with beer addled brains and screeching kids. Bugger it. I was tired, it was another twenty odd kilometres to the next hut. I was staying. They would just have to accommodate me.

You have no idea how relieved I was to discover I'd once more jumped to conclusions. It was a team of volunteers, busy painting, sorting and tiding the hut. Clearly they didn't expect me. Apparently it was on the website that the hut would be under repair that weekend and not open to walkers. I didn't have internet. No, that's a lie. I did have internet, I just never bothered checking it.

In a few short minutes we'd got things sorted out and I was given room in the hut. More importantly I was given tea and a huge slab of utterly delicious carrot cake. Even more importantly later that evening I was given not one but two refreshingly cool beers.

I've already mentioned I'm not really a people kind of person. I might add I'm generally quite shy and retiring, not prone to public outbursts. In this case I overcame my natural reticence.

Late that afternoon, before most of the volunteers left, their work completed, I made a little speech, thanking them on behalf of all walkers for the work they did, the shelter and comfort their efforts provided. It was genuine and heartfelt. Those volunteers do a wonderful job. I thank you all again and not just for your selfless work and contribution–the carrot cake and beers were pretty damned welcome too.

I'm a smoker, neither ashamed nor proud about it. To some it's a weakness, a vile habit. To me it's a pleasure. Being a smoker it's rather obvious these days just how the habit is perceived. Things have changed hugely in my lifetime and what was once a social norm is now considered by many to be abhorrent, the likes of myself feeling as though much of the world would prefer we carried a bell which we rang as we walked down the streets calling out 'unclean,' 'unclean' all the while. Lepers, nothing more, shunned and segregated. I've been to social events where people imbibe gin and whiskey, beer, wine and vodka, often in large quantities, occasionally openly criticising me for my personal habit and the need to feed it. I've yet to hear about a car crashing into a bus shelter full of school children because the driver had enjoyed one too many cigarettes that day; or of a husband going home and beating his wife because he'd smoked too much. But such is life and aware of current views I do my best to ensure when I do indulge my habit I do so without encroaching on other people's delicate sensibilities. It's only being considerate.

At one hut I was joined by a middle aged couple, a nice enough pair. I ate early and it being a chilly evening I wormed into my down cocoon and settled to read for a while. The couple sharing the hut decided to utilise the fire pit provided and enjoy a bit of a blaze rather than hit the sack so early. Sadly their fire building attempts weren't overly proficient and soon the hut was filled with plumes of dense smoke which came and went with the breeze and the addition of more green wood being thrown on the fire. In truth I didn't really mind this. If nothing else it kept the mozzies at bay though at times it did make the eyes water a bit.

During the night the lady of the couple went out for a pee and on her return deposited her used tissues or toilet paper on what remained of the still smouldering fire. For the next twenty minutes the hut was filled with the rather acrid stench of smouldering tissues. Again no worries. It wasn't intentional, she probably just didn't think, and she was disposing of waste in the best way.

I was up early the following morning and having eaten breakfast I took the remains of my coffee to the outside picnic table where I could enjoy a cigarette away from the couple who were still in their sacks. The early morning breeze had changed and was now blowing in my favour, from the hut to the picnic table. No sooner had I lit up than the woman began to cough rather pointedly. The usual happened and I felt my annoyance begin to ruin the beauty of dawn with rising sun slanting through karri trees and birds beginning to give full song. There was no way any cigarette smoke was entering the hut. I was sat metres away with the gentle breeze wafting my smoke off into the forest. It was the mere fact I had the audacity to smoke in proximity that was the problem. I ignored it. The coughing became even more pointed. Finally the lady in question asked me to move away, my smoking was bothering her. Give her credit, she didn't claim it was the smoke bothering her.

Considering all the other very serious troubles in this world we live in today I feel it's a rather poor reflection on current society that future historians will look back at this period and consider smoking to have been a–if not the–major social issue.

On one section of the track I shared huts for a few nights with another European girl, this time a very laid back and pleasant character.

Bee was doing the walk solo but had previously teamed up with an Australian guy I'll call Jo. They'd travelled together for quite a while and had separated only recently when Bee chose to take an extra rest day while Jo continued with the next section. He was now travelling a day or two ahead of us. I liked Bee. She was easy company, interesting and open minded, chatty without being intrusive. She slept in her own tent–pitched outside the hut–and liked her own space which I endeavoured never to invade. I was impressed when she told me she'd attempted the Pacific Crest Trail–a walk that is truly hard yakka–but had failed primarily due to time. The mere fact she'd attempted it and had no shame about failure told me a lot about her, made me admire her more. Bee also smoked so there was no need to disappear out of the hut and away from delicate sensibilities when either of us wanted to indulge. From early conversation I'd guessed that Bee and Jo might have more potential than just walking companions. It was one of those things that crosses your mind but you never comment on or pursue. It's personal and not your business.

On the morning after the first night we shared space I was up and gone before Bee emerged from her tent. I like to walk by myself and as usual I enjoyed my day of solitude. When I arrived at that night's hut a fire still smouldered in the outside fire pit. It was a Monday, the hut was close to a jeep track. I assumed some locals had been there and only recently departed. It was a lovely spot with a slow deep river only metres away where you could swim or just splash around if you had kids. For whatever reason I decided that a family had driven there and spent the weekend.

Once I'd sorted my kit out, washed my socks in the river and taken a brief refreshing swim I went to sign in. The hut log book was in a box bolted to the wall at chest height. On top of the box lay two hand rolled cigarettes, each with a filter and each neatly twisted at the end to prevent the tobacco from falling out. They looked like joints. What the hell were they doing there? Who leaves things like that lying about in the middle of nowhere? Once again I came to the conclusion a local family had camped at the hut for the weekend, enjoyed the solitude and the swimming and the nature. I imagined the father enjoyed a smoke, drove a ute. He couldn't role a cigarette–or a joint–while driving, especially with the kids on board, so he'd rolled a couple for the journey home but accidentally left them behind. What a bonus! Almost guiltily I picked one up, examined it, sniffed it. The tobacco had an unusual odour. I put it back down. What would happen if the owner of these items discovered his loss and turned around to come back and get them? I filled out the log book, replaced it in the box, took another look at these two little items of desire. Why the hell not I thought. His loss my gain. I was restricting myself to only five smokes each day so anything extra was very welcome.

Sitting at the picnic table I lit one up and took a tentative drag. The smoke was aromatic, that's for sure. Strong but pleasant tasting. I waited for a hit but nothing happened. Another tentative drag. Still no hit. It was a plain and simple cigarette and with a touch of relief and a lot of delight I smoked it to a stub.

I brewed some coffee, ate a couple of biscuits, then feeling like a thief I retrieved the second roll-up from where it lay on the log book box and lit it up. What a truly delicious smoke.

Bee arrived an hour or so later and joined me at the table where we chatted for a while before she disappeared to erect her tent. As she was doing this a school group arrived. Rain was beginning to fall so I explained to their guide and the teacher I had no problems with the group occupying the hut, they were welcome. All thoughts of those two cigarettes enjoyed earlier left my head, I never mentioned them even when Bee and I sat to eat together.

The following day rolled out the same as before. I rose early while the school group slumbered on. I was gone before Bee emerged from her tent.

I reached that night's hut by early afternoon, hot, tired but happy. I dropped my pack, rubbed my shoulders, stripped off my boots and socks and sat curling my toes in the sand for a while. I sorted my gear out, put water on the boil for coffee, turned to find the log book and low and behold sitting on top of the plastic box were three hand rolled cigarettes, all identical to the ones I'd found the previous day. This was confusing. Just what the hell was going on?

I inspected each one carefully. For sure they were of the same style and tobacco as yesterday's. I lit one up and smoked it while the water reached the boil. I smoked a second one with my coffee, still amazed but delighted with my find. And then it dawned on me. Guilt ensued.

Bee arrived an hour or so later and once she'd dropped her pack and sat down I asked her if Jo had smoked. Yes he had. I asked if he rolled his own or smoked tailor made. He rolled his own. I asked if he smoked unusual and quite aromatic tobacco. Yes he did, White Ox if she remembered correctly, quite strong and very distinctive. Oh dear. Deep guilt.

I produced the remaining cigarette and laid it on the table. For sure, it was one of Jo's. I confessed my sins. Bee thought this hilarious, my shame even more so. It materialised she had found a single cigarette the first night we shared a hut but hadn't mentioned it to me, just recognising the style and tobacco and thinking Jo had left it behind by accident. The second night I had found two, this being the second night of that section. The third night three, the third night of the section. He was leaving her a cigarette for each day of that sections walk–or for each day they were apart.

Sure enough, the following night there were four neatly rolled cigarettes awaiting Bee's arrival at the hut. I declined from smoking any even though I reached there before her. She was generous enough to share them with me when she arrived. As we chatted I casually mentioned I suspected Jo may be a little more taken with her than she realised, that I saw these cigarettes as tokens of affection. She didn't say much but the following morning she was up before me and departed early, announcing she was going to double hut to the next town, reducing her remaining time on that section from four days to only two, this in the hope of catching Jo before he moved on. She already knew where he would be staying. I wished her luck, quietly delighted love–or if nothing else lust–might be in the air.

I continued alone, perfectly happy with the situation. In each of the remaining huts I used there was a cigarette awaiting me. Thank you Bee–and Jo, I hope it worked for you both.

As an aside, nothing whatsoever to do with the Bib track but still on the topic of people and how we behave, here's a little story that makes me think not just about other's behaviour but also about my own.

During my two months on the Bib I had a lot of down time which I generally filled with nature watching and books. I read several during the walk.

One of those read was 'Blue Desert' by Charles Bowden. The author liked to experience things for himself before writing about them and in order to get a true picture of the hell illegal immigrants from Mexico underwent in an effort to enter the United States he opted to walk one of their trails, seventy miles through the desert. At one point during this walk he came to Tule tanks, one of the few waterholes along the track, one that has been used for thousands of years, first by nomadic Indians, then by explorers and prospectors, now by Mexicans desperately walking north in the hope of a better life. The tanks were dry but stashed in the rough stone wall of a nearby shelter was a steel water canteen. It looked like something left there for the next thirsty traveller desperately in need of a drink. The author dug it out, could tell by the weight it was full. He unscrewed the cap and poured a little of the clear liquid onto a rock where it fizzled and bubbled, hissed and smoked. It was hydrochloric acid.

Are you horrified? Left speechless? I was. I couldn't believe what I'd just read. Couldn't believe anyone could do such a thing, do it intentionally, with the desire to hurt maim kill. Can you imagine being parched, totally dehydrated and coming upon that thoughtfully left steel canteen of life saving water? Can you imagine the thrill, the excitement, the relief? Can you imagine the fulsome weight of it in your hands, the sweet music of splash and gurgle as you lifted it to your lips ... the searing life destroying gut eating destructive agony of that first greedy gulp. Dear God who I don't believe in—who could do such a thing? Who would do such a thing? It brought tears to my eyes, truly. It's doing so again as I write this. What have we become that one person can do this to another ... and for what reason?

Enough.

Soon after completing the Bib I met up with an old girlfriend in Perth. Shaz is one of the brightest, most astute people I know. She has a sharp tongue and an even sharper brain. She can at times make me feel rather like a retard with a speech impediment. During conversation I detailed the horror story mentioned above. Shaz barely batted an eyelid which left me a touch confused. I had found the tale horrific.

A while later I told her about Bee and Jo's cigarette gifts. Shaz didn't seem to find it funny at all. When I'd finished she reminded me of my tale about the canteen left at Tule tanks in the desert and said that's how she would have regarded those cigarettes I smoked. She wouldn't have touched them with a barge pole, immediately suspecting there was some ulterior and malicious intent behind them being left there.

In ways I can understand her attitudes. Shaz has seen a lot of life, not all of it good. But I'm happy being me. I don't want to take off my rose tinted spectacles, don't want to see the world through different eyes, don't want to see it the way some others do.

I sometimes question what that says about me.

Lost and Found

I'll begin here by reiterating this is not a guide book. I'll happily confess I am no expert when it comes to navigation. I have several friends who will enthusiastically confirm this. Little more than a year back from when I write this I got LC and myself a touch lost in my home country of Scotland–and in reasonably familiar territory as well. We did climb a couple of Cuillin Ridge mountains that day–just not the ones we set out to climb. That's fact. We were half way up the first mountain before I realised it wasn't the one I thought it was. How did I manage that? Effortlessly it would seem. Just wandering along, hands in pockets, head full of butterflies and birds, on ground I'd covered only a few weeks previously and therefor believed I knew. Very basically, I was so confident I knew where I was, where I was going, I didn't bother looking at the map. Simple as that.

So dear reader, take from this chapter what you will. I'm simply detailing what I did and the reasons for doing it my way. I'm not suggesting for a moment anyone else follows suit.

When I first began walking much of the navigation was done with little more than common sense and luck. I must have had a lot of the latter and amazingly I survived. This was in Scotland where the horizons can be glorious and distant one moment, then totally non-existent the next, vision obscured by pea soup mist or white-out snow. Yes, I got lost, several times. The fact I'm writing this proves I also got un-lost. The more adventurous my walks became the more I learnt. Map and compass became mainstays. I've never graduated to GPS though I have used it many times while working on wildlife surveys and conservation projects where accurate data is required. I know how to use it, I'm just not a great fan. GPS has too many moving parts. Even more importantly from my perspective GPS–like much of today's convenience technology–stops you thinking, it does the thinking for you leaving you reliant upon it. I prefer relying on myself. I'm old school and perfectly happy with it.

There are all kinds of navigational aids available, ranging from traditional map and compass to off-line apps. It's not for me to advise you what to choose or how to use it. The only suggestion I would make is that no matter what choice of navigational system you decide upon make sure you are fully familiar with it before ever setting out on the track. Practise with it. If you opt for the maps then familiarise yourself with them. Take them out of an evening, have a good look at just one section, get a picture of it in your head, learn what the symbols indicate, how contour lines work, learn to understand what the map tells you. This familiarisation will not only pay off in the long run, it's also good fun and builds anticipation and excitement for the walk. Maps are wonderful things and just taking them out and playing with them can take you away from humdrum existence and place you out there, on the track, even if just in your head.

I like maps. Maps are what I'm familiar with, what I grew up with. Looking at a map gives you an aerial picture of your walk and being a simple soul I like pictures, like to see where I've been, where I'm going, and most importantly where I am. I believe maps are good for all of us, they provide reference to location in a big picture way and we all appear to like to know where we are. We use watches in the same way. Watches give us reference to our location in the day. If it's 10am it's probably coffee time and we know we are roughly a quarter through the working day. If it's 4pm then chances are the wife is picking the kids up from school. If it's 5.30pm then chances are hubby is on his way back from work, battling the evening rush hour traffic, soon to appear in the driveway. If you wake up in the middle of the night do you not check watch or clock to see what time it is? Even when LC and I were parted by thousands of miles, her in Australia, me in Africa, I could tell where she was in her day simply by looking at my watch and adding 8 hours. That made me feel good, gave me a little smile. We all seem to like knowing where we–or our loved ones–are in the day and watches provide a reference. Maps do the same for location on the ground.

Before setting out on the Bib track I looked at all that was available, everything from map and compass, through guidebooks to GPS and apps. I kept it simple and stuck with what I knew. Good old map and compass. Cheap as chips, durable and reliable, light to carry and don't take up much space, don't need batteries or chargers or leads, don't require signal or good atmospherics, less moving parts so less chance of failure. Never once did I get lost. I did become confused on a few occasions but this was always my own fault and generally rectified with little time lost. I tried to take a very level headed and practical approach to the whole thing–more or less as follows.

The Bib, starting in Perth as I did and finishing in Albany, travels in a generally southwards direction for much of the time. When you arrive at the ocean you turn eastwards and providing you keep the sea on your right you're going in the correct direction to hit Albany which is a large town parked right on the coast and therefor difficult to miss. That's the basics. South for a long time, east for a while, bump into Albany.

The Bib is also, for much of its route, quite heavily forested so your horizons are limited, you can't see very far. Taking compass bearings wouldn't be an option or even necessary, but a compass would give accurate idea of which direction you were heading–should you have doubts.

Being forested, being quite heavily used and also maintained, chances are the Bib track was generally an obvious pathway, difficult to miss in a forest environment where vegetation is often dense. In other words if I found myself crashing about in thick bush then chances are I was no longer on a path.

Finally, the Bib track is way-marked at regular intervals with hard to miss little yellow triangular signs generally angled in the direction you should take, especially at junctions.

Add all the above together. From Perth–Kalamunda to be exact–you head roughly south on a well marked forest path until you hit the ocean. When you hit the ocean you turn eastwards (left) and follow more well marked paths along the coast keeping the ocean on your right until you hit a large town called Albany. End of walk. Sounds simple doesn't it. It is simple–providing you are aware of your location at all times. If you don't know where you are then chances are you're lost. Simple as that.

So how do you know your location at any specific time? You use your map, your GPS, whatever navigation tool you've opted for. A wrist watch can also play a major part in all this.

When I arrived at a hut and sat to scribble loose notes for the day I'd take the map out and have a good look at the following day's section, getting a mental picture of it. At times the track deviates from the southerly direction, taking you west for a while, occasionally east for a while, on the very odd occasion you dog leg back north for a short section. Knowing roughly what to anticipate is a good thing. I'd do exactly the same the following morning while enjoying coffee and a cigarette. I'd take a look at the map but this time I'd note the first major junction or change in initial direction on the track, any noticeable feature I could use as a reference point–in GPS jargon a waypoint. The width of the top of my thumb was roughly equal to one kilometre on the map. I'd use this to very roughly measure the distance from where I currently sat until the first major whatever, be it junction or change of direction or river crossing or road crossing. Let's say I measured a rough 4 kilometres. This would take me about an hour to walk. When I finally strapped my pack onto my back, took a last look around to make sure the place was as tidy or tidier than I'd found it, make sure I hadn't forgotten to pack anything, I'd also take a look at my watch and note the time in my head. Six o'clock. That means at around seven o'clock I should come to the first junction, river crossing, road crossing whatever it was I'd chosen as a reference point. I'd set off in the same direction I'd been following when I arrived at the hut, pick up a marker and off we go. Every now and then I'd check my watch. When I arrived at whatever location I'd chosen as a reference point I'd stop and take the map out again, repeat the process. What's the next obvious point of reference on the map? Roughly how far from here to there? So how long is that going to take you to walk? What's the time now? So when–roughly–should you get there? Make a mental–or written should you prefer–note of estimated time of arrival and what you think you're looking for. Off you go again.

Reference points can be anything you want, anything you think will stand out, be obvious to you when you reach them. The top of a hill is a good one. When you get there panting and sweating you'll probably breath a sigh of relief and think to yourself 'thank god, the top at last'. Pause for breath, take the map out and have a look at it. Is that the first major hill of the day? If it is then that's where you now stand, right there on that spot on the map. You know where you are. Road crossings, river crossings, bridges over streams or gullies, stream crossings (but don't always expect water in them even though they are marked blue on the map), power lines you'll walk underneath, a block of commercial forestry with long straight borders. All those pieces of information and many others are there on the map–all you have to do is be able to read it correctly. None of it is rocket science or black magic, just familiarity and common sense.

It doesn't matter what method of navigation you've chosen it will only be of help if you know how to use it, and it will only be as good as the person operating it. Familiarise yourself with it, ensure you understand it and know how to make best use of it. Use it regularly on route so if nothing else should you become lost you'll at least know where you were an hour or two hours ago rather than simply knowing you spent last night at whatever hut it was.

Once you've settled on your choice of navigational aid probably best just to leave it at that, don't go buying back ups, alternatives, arming yourself with a plethora of other equipment. The more you have the more confusing things will be if you do become lost. Stick to what you know, keep it simple and trust it. I can't speak for GPS, I tend to distrust anything with lots of moving parts and giblets I don't understand, but if you choose to use a compass, if only to verify direction, then trust it. Unless they are next to large lumps of iron compasses don't tell lies. In moments of doubt or stress or panic our brains do.

If you are a complete novice, don't have the vaguest idea about navigation, especially in more remote areas where there are few roads and bugger all road signs, then best get some professional tuition, get some lessons. Either the Bibbulmun Foundation or your local outdoor shop should point you in the right direction. If worst comes to worst, teach yourself from books or the internet and then practise until it becomes second nature.

If you do use navigational aids, know how to use them and use them regularly, then you should always have a reasonable idea of where you are–which means you're not lost.

Though the Bib track is well marked there is chance of confusion here and there; some markers are more obvious than others; some are more recently placed than others, still clear and bright yellow rather than discoloured and faded or with tree bark overgrowing them; some are obscured by recent vegetation growth–but they are there, all you have to do is keep your eyes peeled. Within a few days on the track this becomes second nature, you should find yourself wandering along, enjoying all that surrounds you but still keeping half an eye out for markers without consciously doing so.

I became confused on several occasions. I suspect most people do. It's expecting a lot to walk one thousand kilometres without making the occasional directional mistake. Again none of this is worth getting your knickers in a twist over. Keep calm, have a laugh at yourself and if after looking at the problem cooly and calmly you're still convinced you've gone wrong somewhere, retrace your steps until you pick up the markers again. If you've been half awake up to that point then the spot where you went wrong can't be that far away. Probably behind you.

Markers are funny things. Their benefit is they make navigation easy and provide regular reassurance—confirmation you are on the right path. They help avoid confusion at junctions, make the job simple. Against that they stop us thinking, we become reliant on them. The moment you lose them you don't know where you are other than no longer on the right path. That's where your map, GPS, whatever, become important. If you've been using them in conjunction with the markers you should have a reasonably accurate idea of where you went wrong, where you are now, and how to get back to where you should be.

Until I began walking in Australia I'd never had much experience of markers. All I'd ever used was map and compass, often—especially in desert or featureless areas, or when visibility was poor—simply walking on a bearing for much of the time. There are places where stone cairns—built and added too by previous walkers—aid navigation, especially in tricky situations where there may be only one safe route on and off a high ridge, or where a plateau is flat and featureless and a nightmare in thick mist. In certain parts of Europe rocks are splashed with brightly coloured paint to aid navigation through difficult and confusing areas. Regardless of these man made 'signs' you still have to rely heavily on map/compass/GPS/ ... most importantly on yourself. To set off gaily into the bush, the desert, the mountains and expect someone else to be responsible for your navigation is asking, and expecting, a lot. Fact is it's downright irresponsible.

Frequently in huts I'd spend time reading other's comments about their day, their views on the track, hut, etc. Often there were complaints in regards markers. Some people suggested there weren't enough markers, or they were confusing at such and such a place, they needed renewing, they were too high or too low. I've already happily admitted there were times I did become a touch confused, missed markers and had to retrace my steps for a while. In each and every case the markers were there, where they should have been, the fault lay entirely with me.

In the Pingerup section the markers were few and far between but there was good reason for this. You were walking on an old jeep track with no junctions, no alternative routes. This went on for kilometre after kilometre, the track winding it's way through thick bush and swamp, no other track joining or leaving it. If you turned right or left off the track you would find yourself waist deep in thick vegetation or up to your neck in mud. Yet people complained ... there weren't enough markers. I have to ask myself what do people expect?

I think that's my main concern with markers. They take the onus off the individual and we come to depend on them too much.

Safety Equipment.

This is a hard one for me. I've already stated I'm old school. I'm of the view that if you get yourself into difficulties then it's down to you and no one else to get yourself out. I don't like the thought of others risking life or limb to extract me from some mess of my own making. Those others, those strangers, are not responsible for me or my actions or the eventualities of those actions. I am.

Those are my personal views. You are entitled to your own. Take advice from the Bibbulmun foundation.

So no, I didn't carry an EPIRB nor any of the other location devices so easily accessible today. I did carry a phone but seldom switched it on while on the track, only using it during rest halts in town. I did have back-up in the form of my brother in the UK and my sister in South Africa, both of whom insisted I remain in contact and inform them of my progress. I complied with their wishes but only for their peace of mind. I would have been perfectly happy without their concern. Amusingly enough there was one brief moment of minor panic which once more illustrates the kindness of strangers.

Phone reception from Donnelly River is not good and having tried to get a couple of text messages out and failed I shut my phone off feeling confident no one would panic for a few days if they didn't hear from me, by which time I should be in Pemberton and able to contact them once more. No worries. But my sister in South Africa did worry, bless her cotton socks. She'd been following my progress on the maps provided on the Bibbulmun Foundation web site. She knew when I was due in Donnelly River. When she didn't hear from me she waited 24 hours before searching the internet and finding a phone number for the reception at the holiday camp. She called. I have no idea who she spoke with, all those I met there were nice, helpful people, it could have been any one of them. Whoever she did speak with not only remembered me personally but took time to check the register and reassure my sis I had been through on a certain date but only spent the one night there. All being well I should be in Pemberton by whatever date. If my sis didn't hear from me then she should call Donnelly River once more and they would inform the correct authorities, get things moving. How sweet and considerate. I often wonder if it was the lady called Sue who my sis spoke with and she remembered me because I was the cheeky bugger who'd scrounged a couple of beers from her.

So, by all means organise yourself some tracking device or back up, it makes sense to do so, to have a safety net should you fall. It also allows others who may worry about you to sleep easy, and allows them to be part of your little adventure, even if just vicariously.

I did carry a first aid kit, but it was tiny. Anti-inflammatories/pain killers, a roll of Elastoplast and a role of micropore tape. Sometimes when I look at the medical kits others carry I quietly wonder if they anticipate having to undertake DIY brain surgery somewhere along the way.

It's each to their own. You will know better than I what you might need. I'm fortunate in that bites and stings don't appear to bother me and cuts heal quickly and cleanly. I do suffer back problems on occasion and that was the reason for the anti-inflammatories. I used the micropore to fix a hole in my sleeping bag and patch up another walkers blisters, the blister kits she was carrying not remaining in place for more than a couple of hours. I used the Elastoplast to tape up a tear in my backpack. That was it. I was fortunate.

If you are trying to put a first aid kit together then think logically. You are going to be walking so feet, knees and hips are going to take a pounding. You're going to be carrying a pack, heavy at times, so your shoulders and back are going to be under stress. You're going to be dealing with open flamed stoves and probably non-insulated handles on cooking utensils. There will be boiling water in pots. You will be drinking water from rainwater tanks. You're going to be outdoors, at times walking through thick vegetation, exposed to biting insects at others. All food for thought.

Against this it's highly unlikely you're going to injure yourself so severely you cannot make it through to the next town where there will be a pharmacy, a doctor should you need one.

Probably the most common problem is—understandably—feet. All I can say here is that if you do begin to develop hot spots or blisters stop immediately. Don't persuade yourself you'll be fine until the next rest halt or the hut that night. Stop as soon as you begin to feel discomfort and attend to things there and then. Delaying will only increase the problem and the time it takes to heal.

A Sticky Affair

I took a rest day in the town of Collie, staying in the small hotel across the road from McDonalds, but not for that reason. It was cheap and cheerful, popular with walkers, had pleasant and accommodating owners. It was next door to a pub that did excellent steaks. What more can I say?

The hotel had a communal siting room with tea and coffee available. In this room was a large built-in cupboard filled with items left behind–generally intentionally–by previous walkers. I was invited to take a look and help myself to anything I wanted, the cupboard was full to overflowing and required emptying.

Most of the stuff was food, old maps, paperback books, excess cooking items, half empty gas canisters, unwanted clothing, even a couple of pairs of socks. I did find myself wondering who had bought a 2 kg bag of powdered mash potato then only removed a small portion, leaving the rest behind.

At the back of the cupboard I found not one but two walking poles. These were a matching pair of three section telescopic poles with cork handles, adjustable wrist straps and still healthy tungsten tips. They were carbon fibre, light in body, heavy in price. Only one of them was broken, the other in perfect working condition. I took it with me when I left.

I've never really been a fan of walking poles, frequently finding them more of a hindrance than a help. When I first began walking nobody used poles but by the mid 80's everyone appeared to require them even if only to take up space on the side of their packs. They became de rigueur, a necessary item of uniform identifying you as a walker. I'd never used them, never felt I needed them, didn't see why that should change simply because everyone else appeared to suddenly require them.

In the mid 90's, just before Christmas, I walked into an outdoor shop, hustling to do some last minute shopping. Isn't it strange how some of us always buy for other's things we'd like ourselves. I made my choices, took them to the checkout where I was informed I was the 100th paying customer of the day and for this rather strange fact had won a pair of boots and walking poles made by a well known company. The boots fell apart within the year. One of the poles still exists today though in fairness it has seen little use and spent the last seventeen years unused and unloved with a few other meagre belongings at a mates house in Scotland. These poles came with snow baskets and I did use them in winter finding they increased balance and confidence on long slopes not severe enough to demand an ice axe. Occasionally they saw use during hotter months, but only occasionally. For sure they were of assistance, especially on steep descents where they acted like a third leg, providing additional balance, a prop to lean on while you stepped downwards, saving knees those jarring moments. I seldom used them on ascents and didn't like them in scrambly sections where they proved more hindrance than help. They looked pretty good strapped to the side of my day pack though.

I noted on the Bib most people carried or used poles, generally two of them. I'm not sure what's wrong and what's right. Again it comes down to individual preferences. I can fathom the use of poles on steep ascents and descents but struggle to comprehend their use on flat walking. My hands are usually stuck into front pockets. Occasionally I'll give them a change of scenery by hooking thumbs beneath pack shoulder straps or walking hands behind back at the base of my pack. Each to their own.

The most impressive pair of poles I saw on the walk were hand made specifically for the user by a company over east. 'Bespoke' I think is the current fashionable description. They were four piece, each section connected to the next by an elasticated cord in the same way tent poles are. Being four piece they folded small so could be packed inside a bag for air travel. They were ultra light, made of some high tech alloy used in the aero industry. They were not length adjustable and to my mind this limited their functionality. They would be fine on relatively level terrain but when it came to steep uphill where you want to shorten pole length, or steep downhill where you want to lengthen it, their usefulness would be limited. On steep downhill I thought they may even be a liability, enticing you to bend forwards over the slope with a heavy pack on your back. The guy who owned them was clearly proud of them, displaying them happily and telling me all about them. They were beautifully made and unbelievably light. Their cost in dollars was around one third of my total budget for the walk.

I do on occasion—just in the way many other's do—pick up a stick if I think there is a particularly long steep pull ahead. Generally what goes up must come down so the stick will prove useful both sides of the hill. I've picked up sticks all my life and I have no idea where the habit comes from. This happens mainly in woodlands where sticks are plentiful and varied. No sooner have I entered this environment than I find my eyes casting about, looking for something relatively straight, relatively suitable. I seldom use the stick as a walking aid, tending to carry it with one hand, the shaft balanced on my shoulder. Most often these sticks are used for poking, investigating, prodding, parting fern fronds so I can see what lies beneath, turning over other sticks, fishing about in streams. They are more tools, an extension to my arm and hand, than walking sticks. In wet weather or after recent rains they can also be used for knocking the water droplets off vegetation along path sides before your legs get there, this preventing jeans becoming soaked from knees down.

I've noticed others do the same thing, use a stick as a prodding, poking device, a tool. Kids tend to do it as well, especially near water. Could this be something built into our genes, a genetic memory? Instinct rather than learned behaviour? Could it be a leftover from our nomadic days? The stick as a tool which is safer to use than bare hand, a safeguard from being scratched, stung or bitten? Something that will tell you if an animal is down a hole–potential food–without you having to risk sticking your bare flesh in there? A tool that can be used for retrieving something otherwise beyond reach? A potential weapon should you be threatened? I think there may well be some truth in all of this. It pleases me to think that way.

In some of the countries I've visited domestic dogs are maltreated and undisciplined. They tend to gather in packs, barking and surrounding any stranger who dares approach, each animal egging the other on with bared fangs and threatening rushes, The very first thing the threatened stranger does is pick up rock or stick to defend themselves. Wouldn't you do the same?

Many people in Africa carry what is known as a 'snake stick'. These are usually quite long, very straight, de-barked and polished, often with images of snakes curling around them either painted on or burnt into the wood with red hot wire. You can pay quite handsomely for the finer examples, this with the promise that if the stick is carried snakes will not harm you. I'm not too sure about the deterrent abilities of a snake stick but for sure a person carrying a stick in the African bush at least has some form of defence in hand should it be needed.

Westerners pick up sticks as well, the difference being that some tend to form an emotional attachment to them. It's ridiculous really when you think about it, utterly absurd. People with a decent education, a comfortable lifestyle, enough money to kit themselves out with expensive boots and flash waterproof jackets, the time and finance to undertake a track like the Bibbulmun–and what do they do? They pick up a stick, use it for a while, then feel bad about discarding it when they no longer need it. It's true, some people really do become attached to this generally dead, lifeless and inanimate object found lying alongside the track and picked up. How utterly sad.

There they are, happily stumbling along when a hill looms ahead. A reasonably suitable stick is spotted lying close to the track. It's picked up, hefted for weight, tested for length and strength and if deemed suitable a smile forms on the new owners face. As they walk on so the stick is tested, first in one hand then in the other. Bark or small twigs might be removed especially around where the hand feels most comfortable and soon the stick begins to feel familiar. The hill is climbed, the stick a bonus, helping in awkward sections, acting like a third leg and assisting with balance, giving an extra boost on high steps. The area where the hand falls becomes smooth and polished, the grip more comfortable, more familiar. The stick begins to feel like a natural extension. The far side of the hill is descended and the stick proves even more of a boon companion on the way down than it did on the way up. The stick makes things easier, adds confidence, aids balance and softens impact on deep steps.

The day goes on, attachment grows, a touch of affection creeps in. Finally the end of the day or walk is reached, time to discard the stick, return it to it's natural habitat where it will rot and decompose, break down, disappear. But now it's become a friend. It's assisted over all those hours, those kilometres up and down, it's helped keep feet dry providing balance over streams on slippery stepping stones. Its shaft is smooth from the palm of hand, from grip and sweat of nervous fingers. Not once has it failed in its appointed task. No rolled ankles, no jarred knees, no wet feet, no stumbles and falls. How can it possibly be discarded now? It's proven its loyalty, been undemanding, performed it's tasks in exemplary fashion. It's become your ... dare I say it ... it's become your mate for god's sake!

How sad. How pathetic. How utterly, utterly ridiculous.

An educated, intelligent, (theoretically) advanced creature like a human forming attachment–emotional attachment–to an inanimate object like a stick! Dear god preserve us! What hope! It's a stick for god's sake, nothing more. It doesn't know or care who you are. It doesn't love you. It can't even think. It has no feelings! You're not going to break its heart, ruin its life. Just throw it into the bush, let the bloody thing break down and rot just as nature intended!

As if that's not enough–the attachment some very sad individuals form with inanimate pieces of dead wood–then even worse are those who endow the stick with a name, as though it had a life, a personality, had character, as though it were something other than what it really is–just a goddamned stick! How sad is that. How stupid. How totally and utterly ridiculous!

The first stick I picked up on the Bib I called 'Stevo the Stick'. He was a bit of a 'Stevo' I thought, heavy and strong, had a kind of swagger to him, a cocky little bugger, full of himself and ready to prove it.

The second was 'Stick Sticky'. I think she was a girl. Light, delicate to the touch, almost effortless in movement, she had a grace about her many sticks strive but fail to attain, a kind of ballerina beauty ... I hated throwing her away, it ruined my whole evening.

The third stick was ....

A Serpentine Path

Snakes. Come on, admit it, you've been wondering when I'd get around to that one, haven't you. How can you possibly write about the Bib without mentioning snakes? You can't. Everyone loves snakes–don't you? Ok, everyone loves snake stories, especially the scary ones. I don't have any of those.

I've already made mention of the trail markers used to assist navigation, to help you remain on the correct path. These markers are bright yellow and triangular in shape. In the centre of them, painted in black, is an image of the Waugal, the rainbow serpent.

These Waugal markers are sometimes placed on oxide red posts, at others on any convenient item like a tree or log end. Generally, in sections where the path is obvious and without alternatives, the Waugals are about 500 metres apart. At junctions, intersections, bends, or areas where there is a greater chance of navigational confusion, the Waugals are more frequent. By my very rough calculations if you walk the Bib end to end you'll probably see around 2,500 of these Waugals–2,500 snakes. But these are just images, nothing to fear. Fact is you will welcome seeing them. If you're really lucky you may see several of the real thing.

So why do we fear snakes?

I've read we are genetically conditioned to do so and I can believe this. When our forbearers–way back before we'd even stood up on our hind legs–bounced gaily around in the Savannah grubbing for roots and berries, snakes would have been a threat. Many are venomous, the bite sometimes fatal, especially before the days of helicopters and hospitals. Our forbearers may also have been of a size and shape that suggested a pleasant meal. Kind of bite sized chunks, especially to the larger varieties of snake such as constrictors. As years rolled by and several members of the clan had been observed being bitten by a snake then keeling over and dying it will have become obvious to some other clan members that snakes were best avoided. Those who didn't get this message would also get bitten, keel over and die, never to reproduce. Those who did develop a healthy respect for snakes survived and bred, their offspring through the generations having an inherent fear of snakes. Simple as that, or at least that's my take on it. I always was a simple soul.

There are other factors impressing upon us that snakes aren't the nicest of creatures. Most of what we are told is rubbish, nothing more than hearsay, generally provided by those fonder of the sound of their own voices than they are of fact or truth. Generally these people don't have a clue about snakes, have little or no first hand experience and are simply repeating parrot fashion what they have heard from others just as ignorant.

Most of us have, probably from a very early and impressionable age, been party to the world's allegedly most read book. The poor old serpent doesn't get good press in that one, does it.

Those brought up in a rural or snaky environment will also have had impressed upon them from a very early age that snakes are dangerous and not something to be picked up, played with or put in your mouth.

The term 'cold blooded' is used to describe a snake and this aligned with the false belief they are cold and slimy to touch doesn't give them a lot of appeal, especially when compared with 'warm blooded', furry, cuddly, cute little things–like rats.

There are tales of snakes behaving aggressively and even pursuing people. I've never had experience of this though I have seen snakes acting defensively–but only when they feel threatened or have no alternative, no escape route, just in the same way you or I would.

Poor old snake, doesn't stand much of a chance, does it. Nobby-no-mates.

So, it's natural for us to be afraid of snakes, they are a potential threat to our wellbeing and this knowledge could be deeply ingrained in our psyche. But they are not a major threat, by no means a major threat, not something we should lose sleep over or worry about incessantly as we wander along on the path. Snakes are not out to kill you, that would be a total waste of precious and hard won venom, and why waste such a valuable commodity when they can't eat you anyway? Snakes are not going to be waiting in ambush with venom dripping fangs just for you to come along, they are not going to pounce on you from behind bushes or drop onto you from trees–you're not a mouse ... or are you?

Snakes are just as afraid of us as we are of them, and they have every right to be. From my limited experiences I'd say humans kill many, many more snakes every year than snakes ever kill humans.

Snakes will, given the opportunity, get the hell out of your way the moment they sense your presence and probably long before you ever sense theirs. In most cases you won't even know they are there ... or were there. They are gone. Poof! Disappeared. It's quite likely the only indication you will get that there is a snake–or something–in the bush close by is the rustle of leaves as it glides rapidly away to safety.

A lot of our fear and attitude is perception. If I'd written that last sentence *'If you are lucky the first indication you'll get that a snake–or something–lurks in the bush close by is the slow rustle of leaves as it slithers away surreptitiously'* I'd put a different slant on it, a slant many appear to prefer, it suiting more accurately their personal views, this only perpetuating the way the animal is perceived by others.

So, a few facts, the basics.

Snakes are not poisonous. Snakes–or some of them–are venomous. They inject or spray venom. Strychnine, cyanide and some politicians are poisonous. That's not to say you're about to ingest a politician, but we all have to live with their environmental policies. (Come to think of it, these days some politicians often do appear venomous, a case of competition taking precedence over compassion.)

Venom needs to be manufactured and stored by the snake. It's a precious commodity and not something to be wasted. As a means of self defence and a warning, the snake may bite but not envenomate. This is known as a 'dry bite'. I've read that brown snakes can inflict dry bites up to 80% of the time though it's not something I feel any real need to prove for myself.

Snakes don't have ears in the way we do, they can't hear as we can. They can pick up vibration transmitted through the ground via their jaws. This is how they hear.

Snakes don't have the best eyesight. They can detect movement, see shapes but not in great detail. They don't have eyelids, hence the unblinking stare which some people find unnerving. The snake is not fixing you with intent, it simply cannot blink.

Snakes use their tongues to smell, transferring air molecules to a gland on the roof of their mouth, hence the flickering tongue. This is not a threat display and they are not licking their chops in eager anticipation of sinking their fangs into you. They are tasting the air, trying to work out what you are. Due to restrictions with both hearing and sight they rely heavily on this sense of smell.

Snakes hiss by forcibly expelling air through mouth and nostrils. This is not an announcement they are about to attack, it's a defence mechanism, a threat display used to inform you of their presence, that you've entered their space. It's simply a warning. Think of it as a dog growling, telling you to back off. If you fail to heed this warning then you may well get bitten. Think of it logically. If a snake really wanted to sneak up and bite you would it warn you of its presence first?

Snakes are ectothermic. They cannot regulate their own body heat but rely on surrounding temperature to do this for them. Hence basking in the sun or seeking the cool of shade. The temperature around them dictates their body temperature. We are endothermic. We can regulate our body temperature–to a degree but not literally in extreme circumstances. Hence sweating when hot or shivering when cold, we are trying to regulate body temperature.

Most importantly, they don't want to bite you. Snakes will only bite a human in defence, when they feel threatened or cannot escape. If someone stamps on your foot you–without thinking about it–push them away. Snakes don't have arms, only mouths. Given the opportunity they will choose flight before fight.

Of the roughly 3,000 species of snakes currently recognised world wide only 10% are venomous. That's a nice figure isn't it, it kind of makes you breath a sigh of relief, maybe things aren't quite as serious as you initially believed. But this book's central theme is a longish walk in Western Australia and I'm afraid to say Australia is a bit different to the rest of the world–but then again if you're Australian you're probably already aware of this and hopefully proud as well.

Of the current 170 species of snakes recognised to inhabit Australia 100 are venomous. That's 70%. Not such reassuring figures. But look on the bright side Australia, that's another thing you are first at. If it's any consolation the bites of many of these venomous species are not considered fatal for humans.

So how do you avoid getting bitten?

It's simple really. You treat any snake you see as being venomous. 'All snakes are venomous until otherwise proven' should be a good rule of thumb. And you treat snakes–and all other wildlife–with the respect and consideration you yourself would wish to be treated. You leave things alone. Don't interfere.

I've mentioned snakes are ectothermic. They use surrounding temperature to regulate their own. Often they are sluggish early in the morning and require to warm up before they go anywhere. They bask in the same way lizards do. Patches of sunlight, tree stumps or rocks bathed in heat, these are the kinds of places they may be lying. In the heat of the day snakes will often lie in shade beneath bushes. Just be aware.

Stick to the path, keep your eyes open and senses alert. Don't go poking about in thick brush or piles of old sticks. Don't go turning over rocks just to see what's beneath.

There is a surprising amount of surface water along the Bib track. That's a popular place for snakes as well. Water can be a source of food in the way of frogs. It offers quick cooling when temperatures rise. It's a good method of escape. Vegetation is often thick along the banks, this affording good cover. Best be careful around water.

Logs across the track. Don't step over them, you're putting a foot down where you can't see. Step onto them, step off onto the other side.

You can wear protective clothing, gaiters being the most popular items. Ensure they are thick and tough–canvas is good.

Bottom line: The majority of snake bites occur when someone tries to pick up or kill a snake.

In the whole of Australia road traffic fatalities hover around the 1,200 mark each year. In the whole of Australia fatalities from snake bite are now around 2 people each year. According to my rough calculation that means there is 600 times greater chance of being killed in a car in Australia than there is from receiving a fatal bite from a snake. Six hundred times greater risk yet every day we get into those motorised tin cans and pass oncoming traffic at a combined speed of around 220 kph, only a couple of metres separating us, and we seldom bat an eyelid. Yet we worry about being bitten by a snake?

The statisticians among you will point out that many more people drive cars in Australia than go walking, and what's more they do so on a daily basis. For sure I'll agree. The point is driving is a risk we are familiar with, barely think about. It's shifting baseline syndrome. We are no longer familiar with snakes.

Risk management is fine, just be careful not to get so tied up in the whole thing you suffer the greatest risk of all—wrapping yourself in cotton wool and not living life.

As an aside I'll throw an example in here. By no means am I suggesting you behave in similar fashion.

I have a mate who's lived in Tasmania for around 20 years now. He's an avid rock climber and for the first five years he was in Tassie that's about all he did. Tasmania has only 3 species of snake, all of them venomous. I can speak from experience, the Tiger snake in particular is numerous. My mate likes to discover new rock outcrops, put up new routes. This involves crashing about in the bush, generally off-path, forging access. Again from experience, he does this at an unforgiving speed. At times I've only managed to keep up with him by following the noise and the broken vegetation while he all but sprints off over the horizon. He never wears gaiters, seldom wears boots preferring light approach shoes. He's never been bitten.

So how should you behave if you do bump into a snake along the way?

Firstly you should behave with respect, consideration and understanding. You are in the snakes back yard, it's you who's the intruder. Most importantly, don't panic. Stay calm and assess the situation.

There are three scenario's I can envisage–other than the common one of only briefly glimpsing a rapidly retreating snake or simply hearing a rustle in the leaves.

The first is when you spot a snake, on the path, a few metres ahead. Trust me, you'll stop automatically, that reaction is burned into our wiring. Take a breath and assess the situation. Chances are the snake is already aware of you–but it hasn't moved. The reasons for it not having moved could be many. It's cold and sluggish and trying to warm up–snakes, like us, can be grumpy first thing in the morning. It's recently caught and swallowed a large prey and it's trying to digest it–don't you like to sit back undisturbed after a large meal? It's mating season, hormones are rife and it's being ballsy. It's injured. It's just plain ornery. But none of these reasons should be of any interest. The fact is it hasn't moved. Best you do. The snake either doesn't want to move or it's waiting to see where you are headed so it can avoid you. Walk slowly and quietly backwards until you feel at a safe distance. If the snake doesn't take this opportunity to vanish then pause and think again. If the snake was moving on the path when you first spotted it then it's going somewhere. You don't want to go where it was going. If the snake was lying quietly, coiled, then it's happy where it is, there for a purpose and for a while. Use these indicators to choose your own route around it.

Examples: If the snake was crossing the path left to right when you first spotted it and it's now frozen mid path watching you, best you move to the left of the path, this allowing it clear passage on its route. If necessary cut into the vegetation and give it wide berth. If the snake is lying coiled on the left side of the path, head looking out over the path, use the vegetation on the right this keeping you in the snake's view at all times, reassuring it, not going behind it.

The second scenario is when you don't notice the snake until you are almost on top of it. This is a hard one. My instinctive reaction is to freeze momentarily then step backwards away from it. I can only guess I automatically step backwards to display retreat/no threat to the snake while keeping it in view. If I stepped forwards I'd lose sight of it. Freezing is good. It stills the threat. Just don't freeze for too long. Move slowly away–SLOWLY–as soon as possible then assess the situation and how best to continue while avoiding further conflict.

The final scenario. You've stood on the snake. Get the hell off it ASAP. I doubt a snake has the word 'accidental' in its dictionary. What you've just done is an act of aggression. How would you react?

So, golden rules ... be aware, show respect, try not to step on a snake.

The above three scenarios are highly unlikely. The most common encounter is the one you're not even aware of. The second most common is the snake vanishing rapidly into the bush.

My personal experiences on the Bib? If you've got this far then you've probably read the first chapter. What an incredible and unusual experience that was. I still glow inside when I think about it today. Once in a life time I reckon. I'm still not sure if it was me or the snake that lacked something in survival instincts. Probably both of us.

The other experiences. Yes, I probably saw around twelve other snakes, generally just catching a fleeting glimpse of a blackish body disappearing rapidly into thick bush as I approached. I'd lay good money there were very many more snakes that saw me and I was never aware of them. They let me pass unhindered, remaining in cover where they felt undetected and safe.

One other incident involved what I think was a death adder, I can't be totally sure. Although we spent in the region of a minute in one another's close company I relied totally on memory for later identification from a snake book. I'm old enough and ugly enough to understand that getting down on my hands and knees, holding a cell phone or digital camera out in front of me, my attention on the screen and not on the potential threat, is not the brightest of behaviours and though it may win me 'likes' on Facebook it's probably not the best of life choices. I'm also a bit leery of adders.

To call adders lazy is probably unfair. Adders are ambush hunters and tend to rely heavily on their impressive camouflage and total stillness to avoid detection. So confident do they seem about not being spotted they often don't bother moving from where they wait alongside paths for potential prey to happen along. We humans are not potential prey, we are not on the shopping list, but we do tend to wear big boots and often don't appear to care where we put them down. We also use paths, the same paths as adder prey use. This can lead to a bit of a conflict situation. The adder is about the only snake I can think of that even when given ample opportunity to remove itself from the vicinity when it picks up the vibration of those boots hitting the ground, often fails to do so. That's why I'm leery of adders.

The possible death adder in question was small, perhaps an adolescent. It was so small I'd probably have had to offer it my little finger side on before it could have inflicted a proper bite. I noticed it mid stride and froze mid stride. It lay coiled only centimetres from my right boot but it never even attempted to strike. It was still relying on me not seeing it, believing it was still undetected. I stepped slowly backwards and still it didn't budge.

I tapped the ground with my stick. No response. I stamped my feet a couple of times. Not a chance was it going to move. Finally, on the second very gentle attempt, I managed to pick it up mid body with the tip of my stick and lower it into vegetation further away from the path edge. It disappeared quietly the moment it was put back down. It didn't make any attempt to strike my stick when I lifted it from where it lay–either time.

Finally, a couple of other things you may encounter that again appear to strike fear and loathing into many. Scorpions and centipedes.

Fifty-eight days, 1,000 kilometres walked and I was extremely unlucky. I didn't see one scorpion in all that time. What a bugger.

But they are there so be aware.

Scorpion's tend to be night hunters. They like sand, holes they can disappear into, dark corners. They hunt for their prey but often don't wander too far from their day time shelters. Scorpions tend to freeze when your foot falls close to them rather than scuttling away in retreat. They do see you as a potential threat. Wouldn't you feel the same if positions were reversed? They stand facing your boot, pincers spread wide, tail raised, because that is the way they attack prey–and defend themselves. They are not going to rush at you. You're too big. They are just preparing to protect themselves. If you do aggravate them then expect retaliation, generally in the way of a painful sting from the arching tail which can inject venom. To the best of my knowledge none of the scorpions found in WA are considered a threat to humans and there are no recorded deaths from scorpion sting in the state.

Essentially there are two main types of scorpion. Those with big fat pincers and skinny tails which make them look like body builders. These scorpions carry less punch when they sting, relying heavily on their powerful pincers to overcome prey. The other type of scorpion is the reverse having weak looking pincers but powerful tails. These scorpions rely heavily on venom to immobilise their prey so it's safe to tackle it with those weak pincers.

I did see a few centipedes on the track but never at huts. Centipedes are night hunters, often fast moving. Generally they will try and get out of your way. The don't sting but can bite. The bigger the centipede the bigger the bite.

Again, leave things well alone and they won't bother you. If you are concerned then wear enclosed shoes when wandering around camp, especially at night. Put them and your head torch on before stepping out to go for a pee in darkness ... and use your head torch, don't just stagger blindly along. If you're a female best you check before you squat, this saving potential discomfort and much embarrassment later on.

Tick List

I mentioned snakes and you have probably gathered I don't feel they should be a bother to anyone. There's good reason for this. Snakes are often quite large and frequently visible; they invariably get out of your way and you are not on their list of potential dinners.

There are other creatures to be taken into consideration, also for good reason. They are small, often all but invisible. They don't get out of your way—to the contrary they often seek you out. They do consider you a potential dinner item. Some of them are capable of causing minor or major reaction and some of transmitting infection. And you were worried about snakes!

This chapter is primarily about those second mentioned creatures, the ones you might consider bothersome. Ticks, mosquitoes, march flies and spiders.

Walking the Bibbulmun Track north to south, starting in Kalamunda, Perth and finishing in Albany, during the period mid October until mid December this is roughly how I remember things, what my hastily scribbled notes suggest.

From Perth to Collie I encountered ticks, quite regularly. After Collie, none.

I encountered mosquitoes much of the time, more frequently the further south I went, the last sections along the coast being the worst.

March flies were uncommon until Northcliffe. From there south they increased in number, frequency and ferocity, though this latter factor may be influenced by imagination. The coast was again the worst area where at times they verged on being a nightmare.

Spiders were everywhere but shouldn't truly bother you. Spiders don't consider humans as potential food sources and will only bite in self defence. Leave things alone and in return find things tend to leave you alone.

Let's begin with ticks. I don't like ticks, sadly they appear to like me. The first week south of Perth I picked up a few. On the second week I began to pick up ticks every day. I'm told they like to sit in ambush on the fronds of grass trees overhanging the path, ready to attach themselves to anything that brushes past. I can believe this. I know from experience ticks like long grass growing alongside paths, especially just after rain when for whatever reason the moisture seems to encourage their climbing. I also noted that only about half of the ticks I picked up were on my legs, the other half were on upper body. I chatted briefly with one guy who thought the tick sticking out from the back of my knee to be amusing until I pointed out the very large one attached to his neck and protruding like Frankenstein's monster's bolt. I did try using a stick to shake grass tree fronds before brushing past them. I don't think it made any difference. I think you have to accept ticks as part of the walk, for me one of the less enjoyable features of the track.

I'll happily confess I didn't cover up or use any form of protection. I walked in shorts, boots and T-shirt every day. This didn't help but I'd rather be comfortable than almost hermetically sealed into bug repellent clothing, especially on hot days. It's each to their own and many other's encountered along the way wore long pants tucked tightly into gaiters, long sleeved shirts and even gloves, sun hats with insect netting so face and neck were protected. On occasion they still ended up with passengers attached, head buried through flesh, busy sucking up blood.

On a project in Africa, based in an area of primarily open Savannah and bad for ticks, I worked with a girl who religiously wore long pants, leather hiking boots and long canvas gaiters which she sprayed heavily with bug repellent every morning. I wore my usual of light weight boots, short socks and shorts. She never suffered. I contracted tick bite fever twice. This suggests a combination of clothing and repellent is the best way of avoiding problems.

There is no doubt you will be informed by others of all kinds of ways of treating ticks. I was told to use everything from toothpaste to a lit cigarette. I didn't try any of these things. What I did do was use the small tweezers from my Swiss army knife which though not ideal in shape or size seemed to do the trick providing the tick was large enough to get a firm grip upon where its body enters yours. Sounds horrible doesn't it, but that's what you want to do, grip it firmly but gently as close to your skin as you can then apply gentle pressure directly upwards to remove it. Most times this worked. Occasionally it didn't. When it doesn't work the tick's head remains embedded in your flesh and can cause infection, serious itching and quite often a hard to heal wound.

Here's another horrible fact. If when attempting to remove a tick with tweezers you apply pressure to the upper body the tick will regurgitate its meal back into your blood system. Basically it vomits. Delightful. This can cause infection and the transmission of disease–if the tick is carrying.

With this in mind I generally left ticks alone. Often, when I went to check on one I'd spotted the previous night but felt it was still too small to attempt removing with tweezers, I'd find it was already gone. It had dropped out, tummy full, off for a nap then lay a few eggs.

There are also several other tools available for the removal of ticks. In my home country of Scotland where Lyme's disease is becoming common, information centres and outdoor retailers offer free removal tools and a small instruction leaflet. The tool chosen for this free distribution to walkers is a small thin plastic card with two different sizes notches cut into it. The correct size notch is selected, the card slid over the skin and up against the embedded tick until it fits neatly into the notch and then the card is gently used to pry the tick from flesh.

I've never used one. I'm told they are excellent. I believe they are also available through the internet and even some outdoor retailers. Worth an enquiry.

A problem when travelling solo is the limitation on personal body inspection. I'm by no means a supple contortionist and there is only just so much you can see of yourself without the use of a full length mirror, an item I tend not to carry. I didn't really feel it was policy to ask total strangers, especially women travelling on their own, if they'd care to check my body for ticks. Fortunately in some cases, unfortunately in others, this concern appeared to be reciprocal. They probably thought the same about me.

The most common places to find ticks are where clothing meets body; waistbands of pants, top of socks, behind shirt collar if it's worn buttoned. Ticks seem to like tight fitting spaces. Other favourites are where the skin is thin, the area warm and the blood vessels close to the surface; armpits, behind knees, crotch.

In Dwellingup, after I'd booked into one of the walker's rooms, I went to take a shower and while lathering up I noted a tick attached within my pubic growth. I wasn't too fazed and opted to leave it until after I'd showered when I'd try removing it with tweezers. I lathered up fully, rinsed off then repeated the whole thing until I felt clean. I'll add that I tend to take 'army' showers where once you are first soaked you switch off the water and lather up fully, covering every part of your body with slippery suds. You then rinse off. Repeat process. This saves water, saves soap and ensures you are decently clean.

On my second rinse I did note something small and black being swirled around the plug hole before disappearing into it. I didn't think much of it, it had been almost two weeks since my last shower, it could have been anything. I discovered later it must have been the tick. If nothing else that says something about the soap freely available at camp sites.

At some of the huts in the early sections I saw ticks, generally outside, in the sand beneath picnic tables. The huts themselves appeared free of them. Just be warned.

Not only will ticks actively seek you out and feed on you, they can also transmit disease. Fortunately this happens only very occasionally. As far as the Australian medical authorities are concerned the jury is still out in regards the threat from Lyme's disease. I'm neither doctor nor scientist, unqualified to pass comment. I do personally know of one confirmed case of Lyme's believed to have been contracted in Arnhem Land via tick bite. What I would suggest is that you take all precautions deemed necessary for your own peace of mind.

March flies, a personal bugbear.

Allow me to explain something before I begin. I love wildlife, have done all my life. Everything from the huge to the tiny, whether they swim, crawl, glide, stomp, gallop, amble or fly. I'm the kind of person who without thinking will encourage bath trapped spiders onto my hand and evict them out the window; I'll happily very gently pick up wasps or bees and do the same; I've carefully evicted venomous and non-venomous snakes from bath, windowsill, workshop and once from a gas oven–unlit I hasten to add. There are very few things in nature I don't like. I'm trying hard to think of creatures that really don't appeal and apart from the aforementioned ticks all I can come up with at the moment are armoured crickets ... and march flies.

I'm told march flies got their name from early settlers who recognised the creature as being very similar to those found in the UK. Spring in the south of the UK is March/April and probably the time when these insects first began to make themselves obvious, hence the name march fly. The area where I lived in Scotland was much further north, the seasons later, spring not arriving until May so we called them .... 'cleggs'? Go figure. Seasons are reversed in the southern hemisphere, the march fly not appearing until October/November, but the name has endured regardless.

During the late spring and summer months, especially in boggy areas, cleggs could make hill walking in Scotland a bit of a trial. I was never a huge fan of them. It never occurred to me Australia might have something similar in store until I ended up living on a beach right up in the far NW of the country. While sitting out the heat of the afternoon in the shade of a tarp, quietly minding my own business, enjoying a good book, I was nailed on the back of the leg by what I identified as a clegg. I couldn't believe it. Having slapped it hard I noted how it landed on its back in the sand and played possum. By this I mean it was either stunned or just pretending to play dead in the hope pursuit wouldn't happen. I picked it up and inspected it. It looked incredibly similar to the cleggs I was familiar with. It was roughly the same size, hard bodied with a flat back and angled wings, longish legs, and most importantly it had an impressively long proboscis sticking at ninety degrees from its rather large head with bulgy green eyes. It was a clegg. Had they followed me all the way from Scotland? Were they really that intent on continuing the persecution I'd endured and they'd enjoyed for years? I did what I usually do with cleggs/march flies. I killed it. There are few things more satisfying in life than watching a small mob of ants carrying off the corpse of a march fly, especially one that's only recently nailed you on some soft and sensitive spot on the back of your leg.

There is one other time I remember actually enjoying the presence of march flies. This was in Tasmania, towards the end of a very hot Three Capes walk, except it wasn't the expensive and well catered Three Capes walk LC and I were doing, it was the cheapskate anti-clockwise Two Cape version, starting and finishing in Fortescue Bay. On the last day of this walk we dropped our packs at the path junction and with only lunch and water in hand headed off to walk to the end of Cape Hauy. It's an impressive place with stunning ocean views. It also has large drop-offs and having become nervous watching all those others taking selfies while leaning over cliff edges LC and I opted to return back down the path a bit before enjoying lunch. We found a nice off-path spot with gorgeous seascape and settled down to eat. The march flies were bad and soon after I'd slapped one from my jeans and it had fallen next to a crack in the rock I was sitting on a skink appeared–possibly a tree skink–moved towards the flat-on-its-back-legs-in-air march fly and in a flash gobbled it up. Moments later I killed another march fly and this time picked it up and dropped it in roughly the same place as the first. Again the skink appeared and quickly ate the offering. Much to our amazement this continued throughout lunch, the skink becoming bolder. By the time I'd finished eating and had sat back to enjoy a cigarette the skink was close alongside me, often on my thigh, happily eating up any dead march fly either LC or I offered it, taking them right from our fingertips. I know you should never feed wildlife and it's something I avoid doing, but in this case it felt totally justified, the food natural. Hard to say who derived more pleasure, the skink or us.

On the Bib track march flies didn't become a pain until just south of Northcliffe. I can't say if this is because of geographical or seasonal reasons. I'd suspect the latter. From Northcliffe southwards they seemed to increase in numbers and ferocity. By the time I hit the coast they were constant companions both on the track and in the huts. There are times you seem to walk through patches of them where you're plagued for several minutes, then just as suddenly as it started it stops. Don't breath a sigh of relief. The whole process will be repeated only a little further down the track.

March flies are the stealth bombers of the insect world. They sneak up behind you, generally at low level, then ever so lightly land on your naked flesh, so lightly you very seldom feel them. They select some soft, tender and usually very sensitive bit of flesh and then they stab it with what feels like a red hot needle. I really don't like them. Frequently after that sudden searing stab of pain I'd lash out and nail the culprit only to find I'd successfully killed the offending insect but it was still attached to me, that long proboscis embedded deeply in my flesh.

The upside of all this is that march flies are very slow and generally easy to kill. This doesn't appear to dent their numbers much but does give a strange and rather perverse satisfaction. But beware, the march fly can and will play possum, lying upside down on its back, legs in the air, eyes closed ... well, kind of closed, or I imagined them being closed ... but they are not closed, the sneaky, deceptive, sly march fly is really watching you through slitted lids, awaiting your departure, chuckling with delight at your stupidity. The moment you turn your back it will right itself, flutter its wings and take off after you once more. Take my advice and stamp on the bugger, several times.

So how do you cope with march flies? Very badly in my case. I'm not sure if they can be deterred with the usual bug creams or sprays, I never used any though it stands to reason they should work. Clothing would be the obvious protection, but again be aware. March flies can and will stab you through light material, I can vouch for that personally. Frequently I'd finish my day's walk by lunchtime, spending the afternoon relaxing on my mattress, reading or writing. In areas of march fly hell this would not be as relaxing a time as hoped. Sometimes it was like the Battle of Britain with whole squadron's of the things flying in formation into the hut. It was as though they knew I was there and exactly where I reclined. Sometimes it was so bad I became paranoid and could only read a sentence before once more putting the book aside and taking a good look around me, sure there were battalions of these things stealthily creeping up on me. There usually were. That's another thing about march flies; some seem to buzz quite audibly while others are totally silent. Needless to say the silent ones are the worst, like a bad fart, silent but deadly. Often I'd lie inside my quite substantial sleeping bag liner and still the buggers would nail me through the material.

Sometimes I'd lie beneath it, the material doubled in thickness and still I'd get nailed.

I think the only way to deal with march flies is to accept they are part and parcel of the walk and try not to let them get to you. For sure their bites are painful and generally not expected but they are not life threatening. If you do allow paranoia to creep in, if you allow their at times almost constant presence to begin to get to you then you're never going to have any peace, never going to enjoy your walk. If you do choose to use clothing as protection then ensure it's either thick enough to repel bites or loose fitting and not against the skin.

The best means of protection I found was a simple wand, usually of eucalyptus, leaves still attached. It doesn't have to be big or heavy, in fact the lighter and easier to carry and swing the better. I'd cut one and use it for several days or until the leaves withered and began falling off. Most times it was simply carried over a shoulder this keeping the march flies off my head and neck. In areas where the flies became a plague I'd swish the wand behind my legs as I walked along. Another tip if you walk in shorts as I did is to tie a light pullover around your waist, the body of it hanging over your bum and as far down your legs as possible. The sway of the material as you walk does deter them though not always. If nothing else it forces the sneaky buggers to attempt a frontal attack and then you can swat them with your eucalyptus wand.

Like all good things, bad things come to an end as well. No sooner did the sun begin to disappear beneath the distant horizon than the march flies would slowly thin in numbers. Within minutes you'd have the hut to yourself. Peace at last, time to breath easy and relax, cook your dinner and enjoy it slowly.

It's about that same time the mozzies begin to appear.

Mosquitoes. Again these can be a pain in the ass and you are likely to encounter them in most seasons other than winter. The only real problem I have with mozzies is their high pitched whining which can keep me awake. I'm fortunate in that they either seldom bite me or their bites have no reaction whatsoever, I can never be totally sure which.

Contrary to what I expected there is quite a lot of surface water for much of the Bib track and many of the overnight huts are situated close to this–not to mention a rather large rain water tank.

Mosquitoes require water for breeding. Inevitably you are going to meet a few along the way. The amount of water a breeding mosquito needs is minimal and even in places that appeared relatively dry they were still present. Water trapped in a plants leaf; a tiny pool in an indented rock, sheltered from the sun and remaining from last rains; an old tin can discarded in the bush; a hole in a tree; anywhere there is still water mosquitoes will utilise it, their only stipulation being the water is still. Depending on species they can utilise fresh, stagnant, even salt water. So yes, you are going to meet mosquitoes.

Not only can mozzies keep some people awake at night, cause painful and itchy bites for others, they can also be a vector for disease transmission. Again I feel this can all too easily become blown out of proportion, people over emphasising the risks, especially to themselves, occasionally to others.

Be pragmatic, take all the precautions you feel required be it mozzie proof tent at night or just a mosquito net over your sleeping bag in the hut; suitable clothing coverage, especially in the evenings; bug deterrent; mozzie coils. It's all available should you wish to use it.

Again I don't suggest anyone follow my own example, I'm simply stating what I did. I walked in only shorts, occasionally wore jeans and long sleeves in the evenings when it was cold. I didn't have a mosquito net. In Collie, as the frequency of mosquito presence increased, I bought some very expensive 'natural' mozzie deterrent. The first night I went to apply it, just as I scooped some out of the jar onto my fingers, a mozzie alighted upon it, its dark body standing out clearly against the white cream. It hung about for a few seconds, had a bit of a poke here and there, then flew off again. Not the most convincing of results and not what I expected. I did try the stuff on several occasions without any apparent effect on mosquito behaviour. I'm not for a moment saying that's common to all deterrents, only the one I chose to buy. I know for sure there are some sprays and creams out there that work a treat, I just wonder what they are doing to you if used regularly.

Mosquito coils work in still conditions, no doubt about that. I was fortunate. In almost every hut visited on the later, more southerly sections of the track, kind people had left half burnt coils behind. I made full use of them while lying reading before sleep. I did on occasion wonder what was worse for me; smoking cigarettes, being bitten by mosquitoes, or inhaling the smoke from mozzie coils.

If you are concerned about mosquito's vectoring disease, here's another example that may help allay your fears and allow some peace of mind.

We've all heard about malaria, what a killer it is. None of the malarial prophylactics work for me, they don't agree with me. I've travelled quite extensively in recognised malarial hot spots, especially in Africa where I've spent considerable periods of time in regions where the disease is a common and very serious threat. I do carry self test kits should I feel symptoms coming on. I've never yet used one.

Before I end this section I'd like to mention something I found delightful about mozzies while walking the Bib.

One of the attractants mosquitoes use to locate their prey—and prey is what we are—is the carbon dioxide emitted when we exhale. Hence the reason they tend to whine around your head at night. They are homing in on your breath and the heat emitted from your face.

But mosquitoes that feed on us are in turn fed on by other things, bats being one of them. Frequently I'd lie awake at night, head torch off, eyes adjusted to the dark, and watch the flittering approach of bats against the lightness of the night sky. They would enter the shelter and hunt for their supper. Every now and then one would fly so close I'd feel the gentle brush of air from its wing beats against my cheeks, against my forehead, hear it as it fluttered gently past my head. I found this delightful. A bat in such close proximity I could hear and feel its fluttering wing beats on my flesh. I was in no danger and neither was the bat, it was just doing what bats do. It was hunting and eating mosquitoes. That latter fact brought a smile as well.

Spiders. Again this is a creature that appears to hold more sway on our imaginations than it's entitled to. For sure they are not the most attractive of creatures–unless of course you're another spider–but they are not out to hunt or harm you. If a spider bites you then it's most likely self defence. You really have no genuine reason to fear them, they mean you no harm.

Very basically there are two types of spider and you're likely to encounter both on the Bib track; web building spiders and hunting spiders. Web building spiders tend to hang around the web in anticipation of something becoming ensnared in it. Hunting spiders do just that, they hunt. You will find both of these in huts where they are of benefit, keeping the flies and mozzies down, occasionally ensnaring larger insects. Leave them alone, they will leave you alone.

If you are using the bed board in the hut to sleep on then give it a good brush off before laying out your gear. Brushes are provided in each hut. Shake your sleeping bag out before getting into it. Use a mozzie net if you wish. I didn't use any bug deterrents so can't say if any of them are suitable for spiders or work with them. It stands to reason they must have some benefit. Be aware of where you sit, lie or place hands. Just be aware generally. If you use a tent keep it zipped closed.

I saw several huntsmen spiders on my walk. They tend to be quite large as spiders go. They are not pretty, not the ideal partner you'd like to take to the cinema of an evening. They probably saw me in same light. Huntsmen do tend to hang upside down from the roof, invariably just above your head. They are not awaiting you to fall asleep so they can drop from where they hang and engulf your face like a scene from 'Alien'. You are not on their menu.

There are red backs about. You can identify their presence by very messy webs which bear no resemblance to what we perceive as a web. Amazingly enough you can identify the spider itself by the red mark on the upper side of its otherwise black back. Red backs enjoy the undersides of picnic tables and benches, dark corners, the undersides of bush loo seats. Be aware. If it gives peace of mind take the small hand brush often available in huts to the bush loo with you. With the door wide open so the interior is well lit have a good look around. Brush off the toilet seat and beneath it, anywhere surrounding it that makes you feel happy. Check inside the toilet paper tube if you wish. Just reassure yourself all is ok before sitting down and enjoying, performance anxiety removed.

If it's any consolation here's another little example that may help allay your concerns. Other than walking the Bib track when I slept in one of the huts every night, without mozzie net or any other protection, I've also enjoyed sleeping out in the open for much of my life. Probably thousands of nights have been spent in little more than a sleeping bag, generally just laid out on the ground. In Australia the only creatures I've ever had joining me were ants. This event was of my own making. I was tired and it was already dark. I didn't check where I was dropping my sleeping bag before getting into it. I can only guess that my body heat suggested to the ants it was daylight–or they just came to investigate the source and discovered me blocking their front door. It only happened once, I learned from my mistake.

LC once spent a night, a whole night, with a ghost crab in her swag. This was on a beach in the far north of WA. The swag must have been left open while she went for a last walk, the crab entering it while she was absent. On her return LC wriggled into her sleeping bag, zipped the swag closed and enjoyed a good nights sleep. In the morning she suspected all was not as it should be and on closer investigation a crab was discovered inside the swag. I often wonder if the crab was as relaxed about the event as LC was.

But back to spiders. On the whole of the walk there was only one time I felt spiders to be a bit of a problem, but not for the usually accepted reasons.

On leaving Denmark the first section of the walk is along the Nullaki Peninsula, starting at Pelican's Point jetty. In the main it's a path along a narrow strip of woodland with the inlet shoreline on your left and a sealed road on your right. This path appears to be hugely popular with spiders–I'm guessing some kind of an orb web spider–which tend to build their impressively constructed and invariably quite large webs across the path, usually at upper body height. Don't stress, if you're alert you'll spot them from metres back, they are generally full of march flies, another common inhabitant of the area. You could, as I did, use a stick to tear through the web before proceeding. After ten minutes of this and probably twice as many major webs I began to feel a bit of an eco-vandal, a destroyer. When you look at these webs they are things of intricate beauty, things the spider has taken considerable effort and more importantly valuable resources to build. By destroying them you are also destroying the spiders means of nourishment–and spiders are mates for god's sake, they eat march flies. It's not recommended you walk on the sealed road, cars use it. I opted to do so rather than continuing along the path destroying webs as I went.

Another reason you should appreciate spiders is because they catch and eat flies, and lets face facts, there is no shortage of this source of protein in WA. Quite the opposite. Yes, bush flies will bother and for much of the route if it's warm weather. How much they bother you is again up to you. They are only flies. Wear a fly net, enjoy your walk.

The Nature of Things

If you are an avid birdwatcher or find mammals and marsupials make you shudder with delight, please don't become over excited by the title of this chapter, I'm not going to start throwing latin names about or discuss in intricate detail some little known but fascinating fact about breeding habits or faecal sacks. I'm not a scientist, don't even consider myself a naturalist. I'm simply an enthusiastic observer of nature, often not even bothering with names, seasonal plumage details, whether a western brush wallaby wears black gloves because it handles priceless artefacts ... or any of the rest of it. It's the big picture I enjoy most, the sounds, sights, smell and touch of nature, of just being out there, immersed in it.

I loved the Bib track, it rewarded in so many ways in regards nature. I've been visiting Australia for many years now and I've travelled quite extensively, especially in the west. I thought I had a pretty good handle on wildlife, what to expect. I was wrong. Especially in the realm of bird song I was blown away, left gobsmacked and utterly delighted. I'd always considered the region I'd lived in Scotland to have one of the best morning chorus's possible. Those I heard so frequently in Western Australia easily matched, often surpassed, anything experienced previously. The forest was alive, joyous, singing with delight at the new day. If that can't lift your spirits then I wonder if anything can. The most prolific birdsong occurred in the central section of the track, according to my notes from Dwellingup to Northcliffe. Not surprisingly this is also noted as my favourite section, the section I would choose to do again if time were limited.

Do I know which birds were singing? Not a clue. I didn't have a bird ID book with me. At times I did regret this but then I thought about the weight and space, the fact I'd also need binoculars, the concentration I'd have to devote to singling out one species, identifying it from the book, listening hard for its individual song. And for what reason? What benefit? To know its name and therefor in a way own it? Be able to lay some claim to it? No, I was perfectly happy just listening, absorbing, wallowing in that celebration, that delicious salute of joy to the new day.

I did recognise a couple of birds, I'm not that much of a numpty. I do know a bit even though I tend to hide my light under a bushel. Emu for instance, I saw several of them. I recognised and could name them instantly, a fact which didn't actually enhance the viewing experience in any noticeable way.

Emu's are wonderful birds, the fact they are relatively easy to spot and identify doesn't detract from this. Size for instance. They're not exactly sparrows, are they. They are impressive even if only for that reason. This size should also make them worthy of respect from even the most disrespectful of walkers.

Early on in the walk I caught up with an adult emu escorting five well grown chicks. Emu's are unusual in that it's the male who looks after the brood. Fact is it's the male that does just about everything (but if you're a bloke don't tell your better half). The male builds the nest then incubates the eggs for around eight weeks barely eating or drinking during this period. When the chicks hatch he chaperones them until they are capable of looking after themselves. This can add up to a year's dedication. And what does the female of the species do while all this is going on? In most cases she deserts her partner, puts on fresh blue eye liner and rushes off to find another male with whom she will mate, again leaving him to do all the work while she once more sassies off in search of yet another potential partner. Like I said, if you're a bloke best make no mention of this. If you're going to tell your partner anything about Emu's simply suggest they make lousy role models. On the other hand, if you're a female reading this I hope you're feeling proud for the good old emu of same sex.

The males tend to be very attentive and protective fathers. I've seen one take a rush at a parked car simply because it heard the electric window being lowered by the driver who had thoughtfully parked well off road and switched off his engine. All he wanted was to take a photo of the adult male emu ushering his entourage of chicks along the sealed road and past the parked car. I was that car's driver. It was an impressive display of aggression and I believe the emu meant business. With this in mind, when I caught up the family group on the path, I resolved to hang back and let them continue before me, sure they would eventually head into the forest and leave the path, allowing me safe passage. And that's what happened though it took almost half an hour of gently wandering along behind them, the father fully aware of my presence and shepherding his brood along before him, until they finally cut right and into the trees. I waited until they were a good fifty metres off track before increasing my pace and passing them. All the while the father watched me openly, head raised and slightly turned, one eye fixed beadily on me as I sidled quietly past. Only when I was well down the path and away from his family did he turn his attentions back to what he was doing, tipping forwards and lowering his head, beginning to search for food as his brood were already doing. It was a nice encounter, neither of us stressing too much about the other.

I recognised another bird only a few days later. The fact is I recognised two birds, both at the same time. Are you impressed? A double whammy. I came wandering over the crest of a rise and there, not more than 30 metres from where I came to an abrupt halt, a wedge tailed eagle was tucking gustily into a parrot in the middle of the path. From what remained of the parrots plumage I'd hazard it had once been of the ring necked variety. What a wonderful sighting. For quite some while the eagle was totally oblivious to my presence. I was terrified to move, amazed I hadn't been spotted immediately and sure that if I did try to move even in the slightest the eagle would pick this up and take flight. I remained frozen to the spot and watched as the wedgie tore into what little remained of the parrot. The eagle held its prey down with one large taloned foot while it tore strips of raw flesh from the body with that wickedly curved beak. It would raise its head, take in it's surroundings with those almost angry dark eyes and once sure all was safe it would point its beak to the sky and gulp the food down with long jerking movements. This done it would again scan the surroundings, clearly feeling a touch vulnerable feeding where it was. Its head would jerk left and right, cold hard eyes missing nothing and only once it felt sure it was alone would it dip its beak to prey and tear off another strip of flesh. Inevitably of course the eagle did spot me, or should I say 'sensed my presence'. I've experienced this before, many times, and often when I've been in a much better place of concealment. It doesn't happen every time but it does happen and it never ceases to amaze me. One moment everything is going swimmingly, the next moment it's gone pear shaped. The animal or whatever doing its animal thing, me concealed by deep shade and often in thick bush, utterly motionless and not making a sound, not a peep. The wind blows consistently from it to me. There is no way it can scent, see or hear me. And then suddenly it freezes, halts what it's doing and goes absolutely rigid as though its just heard the sound of a distant shot. For long seconds both of us are frozen, not a breath between us. Then it will turn its head and look directly in my direction as though trying to penetrate the bush with its eyes. Sometimes this can last for long minutes before suddenly the animal makes its mind up and either vanishes with barely a puff of dust or backward glance; or simply turns and trots off with the occasional halt to stare back once more as if looking to confirm its suspicions. I know for sure the animal has not seen, heard or smelt me. It has sensed my presence, become aware, some instinct telling it it's being observed though it probably doesn't know by what. I'd imagine that way back in our history we possessed the same ability, that sixth sense. Sometimes I wonder just how much we've lost in our relentless search for more.

In this case the eagle didn't even freeze. It simply paused in what it was doing for the briefest of seconds and without even looking my way it took to the air. Survival instinct had kicked in. It had simply sensed things were not right and taken appropriate action. No checking around to find what was causing all those signals to be sent. No hesitation, just flight. Get back into a safe and familiar environment–the sky. For long seconds I watched its departure, half of me sorry to see it go, half of me terrified for it as it drifted down the path, wings at wondrous stretch and beating the air as it strove for lift, the spread finger tips striking path-side vegetation. I worried it might damage itself, immediately feeling responsible though the meeting had been chance and not pre-empted. The eagle gained lift, cleared the understory, began to battle upwards between the thick grey trunks of towering trees. I watched breathlessly, heart quite literally in mouth. Up and up it climbed in a long, gentle spiral ... but ever so slowly, striving its way towards a gap in the canopy large enough to allow it to break through, those impressive wings beating, seeming to claw at the very air, a film shot in slow motion. Just as I was sure it must stall, tumble, return crashing to earth it broke through into the wide open and was whisked out of sight by the breeze, lost above the foliage. I breathed a genuine sigh of relief, found I was beaming ear to ear.

Something else would happen along and benefit from what little remained of the parrot.

Birds are almost constant companions along the track. From first thing in the morning when they greet you with their welcome chorus to the new day, until last thing at night when kookaburras gather and cackle merrily while other varieties give almost sleepy, quite calls as they go to perch, they will be there with you, especially in the forested areas. During the night the occasional owl will hoot or screech; birds I couldn't identify will call softly, their voices blending with velvet darkness. As you will have gathered, though not a 'twitcher' I do enjoy birds and on the Bib I found their frequent presence a highlight. I think if I had to name a favourite–and I don't really like favouritism–it would have to be the Fairy Wrens that entertained me so often while I sat relaxing at a hut in the afternoon, that day's walk completed. I loved their trilling from dense bush, the way they move in orchestrated gangs, hopping and bouncing round the camp as though threatening you by numbers and presence alone, their wonderful shades of blue such a glorious contrast to the browns and greens of vegetation, their movements so light and delicate. How do those legs support them?

Another ten very enjoyable minutes were spent in close proximity to a family of wild pigs. Yes, I know, pigs are not indigenous to Australia–are we? They may have been ferals but they were still 'wildlife' to me. Free roaming, totally wild animals. I liked that fact. I'm also rather fond of pork in all its guises and imagined the wild variety would taste a lot better than domestic pig. Never having eaten feral pig in Australia I can't say for sure but as I watched these animals I surmised there may be little excess fat, the animal hard and lean, the meat a product of natural foods and probably quite 'gamey' in taste, not an anti-biotic, food 'additive' or parasite drench ever passed it's happily chomping jaws and salivating lips. Just good, healthy, naturally produced pig meat, rich and lean and juicy. Delish!

On this occasion I was strolling along when I heard familiar snuffling and grunting. I stopped, froze, listened hard. Several pigs were busy rooting about in a small area of marsh not more than 30 metres away. For a while I stood and listened coming to the conclusion they had no idea I was there and were just getting on with their piggy day. Quietly and slowly I climbed the bank to my right, this to get a better view, to look down on the area of tall reeds and grasses the pigs were in. For the next few minutes I sat there happily watching. I guessed it was a mother with a well grown brood of piglets, all of them happy as the proverbial pig in shit, rootling about and making little squeaks and squeals of delight, communicating their contentment with one another in the thick vegetation. And then the usual happened. In the click of a finger the whole place went quiet, the grass stopped waving with the passage of bodies. It was as though someone had flicked a switch. Seconds passed and again as though a switch had been flicked the whole family vanished with barely a noise, only the gentle swish of grass fronds as they sped off, all in the same direction. How do they do that? How do they know you're there? How do they know which direction to head for safety and all take it like a school of fish, a flock of birds?

This event reminded me strongly of some of the times I've sat and watched families of warthogs in Africa, digging, snuffling and eating, some of them down on their front knees as they graze, a warthog trait. One moment it's business as usual, the next each and every animal is frozen mid chomp, grass or root hanging from corner of mouth, heads up and every sense alert as they try to fathom what's disturbed them and where it is, ears twitching, snouts tasting breeze as they strain to pick up the slightest sign of potential danger. Most times every individual animal will freeze simultaneously as though some message has been transferred instantaneously. Elephants do exactly the same. A moment later the tails will go erect like little radio ariels and the whole family will turn in unison and disappear off into the bush in exactly the same direction. The family of feral pigs I saw that day on the Bib may well have been the relatives of domesticated pigs gone wild but their instincts, senses and reactions were as sharp as, and similar too, any truly wild pig I've seen. That alone was good enough for me. I rose from where I sat on the bank, a smile of genuine happiness on my face. Banishing all thoughts of how nice those feral hogs may have tasted, especially with a side of apple sauce–or maybe even cranberry jelly–I wiped the saliva oozing from the corners of my mouth and continued on my way.

Kangaroos and wallabies were regular sightings throughout the walk though in the more forested northern and central sections these sightings were brief. Frequently I'd be close to these animals before they realised I was there–and generally before I realised they were there. Kangaroos would crash off through the bush for a few metres before halting and looking back as though to confirm there was indeed a reason to make for the hills. Wallabies tended to give only very fleeting moments of sight before disappearing into cover. The most enjoyable day with kangaroos came on the coastal section immediately after paddling across Irwin inlet after a night at Peaceful Bay. The moment you leave the canoe and inlet behind you enter an area of rolling hills, open heathland and pasture. Kangaroos–and emu–are everywhere and either due to familiarity with walkers or the wide open spaces offering clear vision and unimpeded escape should it be necessary, they appear unconcerned by your presence. It was a genuine pleasure to be walking in such an open area for a change and the addition of large numbers of kangaroos happily grazing, dust bathing, or simply lounging around in the shade in that wonderful way they have of lying on their sides like sunbathers around a swimming pool, made the day for me. I'm not sure why but there was a feeling of timelessness and peace to the place, one I enjoyed. I'd put that one section down as the nicest walk between Walpole and Albany.

Other creatures met most commonly along the track were blue tongued and monitor lizards. It's easy to tell the two apart. Monitors, if stumbled upon unexpectedly, will do exactly as you yourself do. They will jump half a metre into the air, turn around and hit the ground running. Conversely blue tongue's will confirm their identity by refusing to get off the track, turning their heads to face you, opening their large mouths widely, hissing loudly and showing you their wonderfully blue coloured tongue. Well, that's how I identified the two of them.

I met several monitor lizards and other than on a couple of occasions the glimpses were fleeting, similar to those of snakes. Little more than a sudden rustle in the leaves and the brief sight of a large lizard vanishing into thick cover. I never pursued. On one occasion I spotted a small monitor about two metres up a path side sapling, clinging to the vertical trunk and frozen mid climb. It was clearly aware of my approach but had opted to remain where it was rather than risk leaping to the ground. Often complete stillness is the best form of camouflage. I never looked at it directly. Many animals are sensitive to this, fully aware of where your eyes are and what they tell you. If they feel their cover is blown they take appropriate action. I walked quietly past, so close I could have reached out and touched it. Another Monitor meeting was a touch more traumatic. Ambling along, head somewhere other than where it should have been, I rounded a corner to spot what appeared to be the world's largest monitor lizard lying in the shade of a bush only a couple of metres away. I'm not suggesting it was Komodo dragon size though that was the first thought that went through my pea brain. What I will say is that it was one of the largest monitors I've ever seen, over 2 metres from nose to tip of tail. It's hard to say exactly as we didn't spend much time in each other's company. We both reacted as described earlier—by jumping straight up in the air, twisting around mid jump and landing with legs already running. Fortunately the monitor lizard's reactions were considerably faster than my own, this saving me the effort of even trying to jump. By the time my instincts were issuing instructions it had already disappeared into the surrounding bush.

Blue tongue's can also give a fright if you're not being observant, but they will warn you with very audible hissing if you get too close. They really don't like moving, probably because they are fully aware they're not exactly olympic sprinters so turning their back on you could be inviting disaster. Step slowly around them giving them as wide a berth as practicable, they are in fear of you.

Before starting the walk I'd read on the internet that rodents could be a problem in the overnight huts, at one point even finding the word 'infested' used. I never experienced this, didn't even find signs of droppings in most of the huts. In only two huts did I see rodents, too briefly for identification. One lived beneath the sleeping platform but never bothered me. Another scuttled about in the rafters for a minute or so after I'd first arrived but was never seen again. Each and every hut has a large sealable plastic box, this for overnight food storage. In one of the huts a corner of this box had been chewed away, a rodent trying to get at the contents. I have no idea what the contents of that box may have been, or what kind of rodent did the damage, but one or both of them must have been quite exceptional because that was the only case of breaking and entering on the whole track. I never used the food storage boxes preferring to ensure everything was packed away in my backpack each night and the pack itself hung from a hook above my head or from the roof supports. I never had a problem. This alleged but never experienced issue with rodents could be a seasonal thing. During the colder, wetter winter months it would be natural for animals to seek good shelter—and convenient food source.

One of the things that surprised for more or less the duration of the walk was the amount of surface water in the way of small streams, forest pools and rivers. I really hadn't expected to see so much water. In some areas a different source of water would be passed two or three times each day. Most of the huts are also close to water which not only results in the presence of mosquitoes but also caters for frogs–not that all frogs rely on surface water.

I would hazard a guess that for half the nights spent in huts frogs were audible, sometimes quite raucous. Fortunately I enjoy a good frog chorus and always found their presence and calling a welcome intrusion to the evenings peace and quiet. They are part and parcel of the bush and a pleasant reminder you're in it.

It's the male frogs that sit and call, this in order to attract a mate. As your ears become attuned you'll note there are often differences in calls. This is simply because there are different species inhabiting the same area. In order to prevent confusion each species has its own song. Listen and you'll begin to pick up the variations.

So how does a lady frog decide which male might be a suitable partner? She listens to his song.

Males tend to find an area with good acoustics, a place which will allow their song to carry loud and clear. They settle in it or on it and begin to give voice in the hope of luring a young lady closer and closer until mating takes place. The bigger and more capable the frog the more likely he is to obtain a good position for calling. The louder and more strident his song, the better it carries, the more ladies he attracts. But nature, as it often does, likes to give the less fortunate a chance as well. Some male frogs, realising they can't compete with 'Big Bill' sitting on top of that lily pad over there, hogging the best location and signing for all he is worth, opt for more devious methods of claiming a mate. Very quietly, very unobtrusively, they sidle, swim and hop over to where Big Bill sits giving it his all. They take up position close by, remaining silent and hopefully completely undetected. When a responsive lady frog happens along, lured by Big Bills love song, they take full advantage before she ever gets to Big Bill. Makes sense I suppose. The scientific term for these opportunistic little fellows is 'sneaky buggers' ... well, that's my term for them. I've known a couple of people who behave in similar manner, New Zeelunder's, both of them.

Sneaky Buggers are common in more species than just frogs and humans. I've seen the same thing happening with Red Deer in the Scottish highlands. The dominant male becomes engrossed in a battle with another male trying to steal his harem of hinds. As the fight for dominance ensues, understandably demanding all the stags attention and often taking him some distance from his harem, another male will sneak in and do the business with any hind willing to remain still for long enough. If you're a bloke reading this you could well be thinking 'that's terrible, she's being totally disloyal to her man!' Not really. She, like he, is simply trying to ensure the continuation of her own genes.

I mentioned feral pigs earlier. WA like most of Australia, has other feral animals which do considerably more damage than pigs. Fox and cat, major threats to endemic Australian wildlife. I've read all the figures, frequently seen evidence of the damage myself. The problem is bigger than Ben Hur. Strenuous and impressive efforts are being made to reduce, even eradicate these introduced predators, many of them now beginning to prove successful.

Nature hates a vacuum and when a predator like a fox is taken out of an area it's short time before another moves in to take advantage of the vacancy. To this end the only way to ensure total elimination of alien predators in a given area is to fence it off, eradicate them all and then ensure no others manage to access the place. It's been proved to work. What you end up with is a patchwork of tiny (in relation to the country as a whole) sealed off havens of balanced and natural ecosystems endemic to the area. In Africa exactly the same is happening. Relatively small areas of land are set aside and fenced off then populated with indigenous species in hopefully about the right numbers and variety to maintain a balance. The incongruity of this is that in Africa the areas are fenced off to stop what's inside getting out. In Australia areas are fenced off to prevent what's outside getting in.

Fox and cat. I saw very little sign of either until I was more or less on the southern coast–and I was looking. The Pingerup plains before Walpole were the first to show frequent sign of both animals. There were regular signs of pig there as well. From Walpole onwards no signs of pig but evidence of fox and cat increased. No sooner had I left the forests and entered the more open heath and scrub of the coastal dunes than I began to regularly pick up tracks and signs of both animals. Twice I actually bumped feral cats on the path and once caught a fleeting glimpse of a fox as it vanished off the track before me. These are just my observations from the walk, I don't know enough to offer explanation.

Though the wildlife encountered along the track was a major revelation and the high point of the walk from my perspective, there were times this could prove a little frustrating. Though I was under no real pressure, no set time limitations, there was still the nagging self inflicted need to just keep going, never to tarry. Added to this were food restrictions dictating I keep going or run short. If it's nature that interests you most and actually doing the walk is a minor consideration I'd suggest you'd be better spending time and money by just going to one of the huts and settling there for a couple of nights, using it as a base to explore the area and enjoy its wildlife. Alternatively you could select a complete town to town section and take double the amount of food required, this allowing you a couple of nights at each hut and letting you explore the area and all it holds. All this is possible on the Bibbulmun Track and all without major expenditure or organisation. It doesn't matter whether you are relatively local to the track or someone from overseas who simply wants a good taste of bush scenery and wildlife, this golden opportunity is there.

Can't See the Wood ...

If you like trees you'll love the Bib. Fact is if you love plants you'll love the Bib.

When I sat and read other's comments in the hut log books the biggest kick I got was reading those left by people who clearly loved plants and animals–nature in general. I enjoyed reading their comments, even if they were simply lists of wild flowers seen along the path or praise to mammoth trees in the sections further south. Reading about someone's blisters or how they were double hutting, exhausted but pressing on regardless, steely grey eyes fixed on distant horizon, really didn't do much for me. Reading the delight someone had taken in their days walk did. After only a few days on the track it became obvious some of those travelling before me were doing that section–or the whole track–primarily just to be out there, the walking almost secondary, nothing more than the best means to be where they were, seeing what they were seeing. This delighted me. In my head that's what long distance trails should be all about; just getting out there and enjoying it. The walk shouldn't be a fight, a major effort, a trial rather than a trail. It should just be fun and comments left in the log books brought home the fact there are many others who walk not just for the walking but because of where it will take them and what it will allow them to experience.

The majority of the walking on the Bib track is through forest–young, old and somewhere in between. Forests can be sensuous things. Forests are a delight. A mix of shade and light, a hundred different greens. Heat and cool. The crunch of pea gravel beneath your boots. Birdsong–nature's music–playing gently in the background. The sigh and rustle of wind caressing high foliage drifting softly down to you.

Forests are beautiful things to walk through, to spend time in. Your horizons may be restricted but your senses will be alive.

The height of spring flower season was past by the time I began my walk but for the first month there were still many colourful blooms along the path. I've been fortunate enough to see mass blooming in more arid and open areas in both northern Australia and Namaqualand in South Africa and though these are impressive in both colour and sheer immensity I found I still got the same kick from finding small patches of rich colour among the forests greens and browns. They were a delight and a contrast, they heralded new growth, the coming of summer, the continuation of the seasons and always they prompted a pause even if only for a few seconds.

Ahead of me for much of the first couple of weeks travelled a few people who clearly delighted in the last of the spring flower display and every night I'd sit and enjoy their comments of excitement as I read of their discoveries, the pleasure tangible in their words. Needless to say I didn't have the vaguest idea what I was looking at when I paused to stare with simple delight, but not knowing the name or species or order of the plant that had caught my attention didn't detract from pleasure.

Not being a botanist I'll keep things simple–always the best way– and split the walk into three sections–North, Central and South–which is how I remember the change in surrounding vegetation.

The most northerly section, Perth to Dwellingup, was primarily new growth forest, the old growth cleared long time ago for the timber trade. I read a few disparaging comments about this and in ways could sympathise and myself feel the loss of those ancient forests. What's done is done and back when it was done few appreciated just what was being done, what was being lost. Our appreciation and understanding of environment and ecosystem grows with each passing year. I often feel that rather than bemoaning what past generations did our energies would be better spent in looking hard at what we do today and plan to do tomorrow in an attempt to pre-empt and possibly avoid further destruction, loss and disaster–and that applies to us as individuals and how we lead our daily lives as well as big picture.

So the old growth forests have gone, been raped and ravaged. What remains? New growth forest, a veritable delight to walk through–young, vibrant and full of hope. You can almost feel the energy around you, the striving for space and light and growth, for life itself. There were times I found myself strolling along and comparing the surrounding forest to an ongoing rave, everything jumping and dancing, celebrating the moment, celebrating being young and alive. I liked those second growth forests. One day they may well be old growth forests.

Most of the forest in this northerly section consists of Jarrah and Marri. There are areas of wattle, open spaces with grass trees (ticks?) and all along the path are orchids and other splashes of brilliant, enervating colour I didn't and couldn't identify, I just enjoyed them.

One of the nicest parts of this northern section is the granite outcrops painted with lichens from rust to grey in colour, the ancient rock warm to the touch when you sit to rest, firm and grippy beneath the soles of your boots as you walk. These outcrops offer space around you, often a delicious breeze to cool your sweat damped skin. I loved them. And hills, yes, I liked those hills as well–but lets be totally honest here. Though western Australians are in ways understandably proud of these up-swellings, in the great scheme of things, when compared to other 'hills' found around the world, they tend to be a bit on the pimplish side. But they are hills nevertheless and not only do they make you sweat, pant, wheeze and gasp, make your thighs and calves scream and your heart hammer, they reward your efforts with often spectacular views which justify all the effort. There are few places remaining in the world where you can stand atop a hill and look out over mile after mile after mile of empty bush. No fences, no roads, no buildings, no people. Nothing but bush for as far as the eye can see. Eyes and brain struggle to cope, to absorb this unfamiliar, wonderfully full emptiness. Drink deep. Feast on it. It might be gone tomorrow.

Dwellingup down to Northcliffe, yes, my favourite section of the walk. There was a lot of up and down, much more than ever expected, but the forests were a delight and progressively becoming richer in diversity of all kinds the further south I travelled.

Jarrah, marri and grass trees still remained but these were now joined by banksia, some unexpectedly already in bloom, their flowers from a distance making me wonder if I were about to stumble on a crop of maize cobs, or a candelabra of red candles. There were patches of mature forest and I attributed these to the increase in bird life, the mixed vegetation attracting a greater variety of species. Just south of Ballingup you spend a little time in pine plantations, mono-culture monotony, but it's still pleasant walking and I quite enjoyed the brief change from natural forest. In the Plonkhole (what a wonderful name) area I saw the first of the paperbarks which would become familiar further south. Mellaluca and flooded gums appeared in this area as well. One of the few trees I could and did identify on sight had caught my attention if for nothing other than its intriguing and quite wonderful name—snottygobble. Who the hell names a tree that? Apparently it's another legacy from early settlers who may have taken a similar name over with them, this referring to the yew berries familiar in the UK. Every time I hear or see the name I think of what some people do with their index fingers when they think no one is looking.

As you enter the Donnelly River area the trees–in places–become impressive in size, probably the area with the first truly big, mature growth I remember. This is karri country, an area once very heavily cropped for timber but still wonderful to walk through. This continues on and off until Northcliffe. Again there were wild flowers along the way but their frequency had dropped off, a mix of locale and season.

The final section, Northcliffe to Albany, is a real mixture of vegetation. Early on you spend several days in the Pingerup plains. Here paper barks are common, interspersed with clump of sheoak, karri and bottlebrush. The Pingerup is more open country, the trees less dense, much of the area wet and marshy with a predominance of reeds and grasses. It wasn't my favourite place though it did offer interesting variation after the weeks of forest and the huts were invariably nicely situated.

From there you head into sand country and the first of the dune and ocean views, the vegetation becoming more open the closer you get to the coast until finally you walk through heath and scrub. I liked this first coastal section where the breeze was good and distant horizons were a complete change from the forest.

From Walpole you head back into the forest for a brief period but this time the domineering view is of tingle trees (another wonderful name to my European ear) which are spectacular if only for their size. It was those which had suffered fire damage that intrigued most and often I'd find myself staring into their fire hollowed trunks and wondering how in the hell they remained standing–but they do. The fires in the past have burnt out the central core of the tree, an area that helps support the tree but not its life. The vascular system used to transport water and nutrients lies just beneath the bark and providing the fire doesn't damage this the tree survives and even continues to grow. Some of these tingles really did look as though they were supported by nothing more than a few thin legs of bark, their centres completely hollow and burnt out so badly you could walk through the tree trunk itself. To say they are majestic fails to do them justice. These southern forests with their array of ancient growth, of towering grey trunks and a canopy so high you have to crane your neck to stare up at it had the same effect on me as oceans and mountains have. They put things into perspective, made me feel small, inconsequential in the great scheme of things which is exactly what I am. Frequently I found myself staring at some spectacular, aged growth and wondering what it had seen, what it had experienced in its life. If only they could talk. I also found these mature forests quiet in ways, almost subdued, the light and breeze often restricted. At times it was as though the whole forest held its breath, as though it waited for something. New growth?

When you leave these wonderful forests it's back onto the coast for the last leg to Albany. Salt air, high winds, sandy soils all contribute to the vegetation growing there. Trees–mainly paperbarks and rather stunted jarrah–only grow in number along old stream beds or in sheltered gullies. It's an area of waist high bush and heath scrub, peppermint and banksia, of stunning ocean and coastal views, of fresh breeze almost every day. Wildlife still abounds and sightings are regular and unrestricted. Much of the birdsong has been left behind in the forest. Now it's black cockatoos with lazy, almost prehistoric wingbeats and raucous calls, pacific gulls with their effortless gliding that take your eye as you wander along. On the shoreline waders rush busily about in front of you, rising to fly only a few metres before settling and running on again. Only in the last few hours before Albany does vegetation thicken consistently, then sand and scrub and tree are replaced by asphalt, brick and mortar.

Best put your plant books away.

Last Steps

I managed to get lost–or become directionally confused–in Albany. For a change this wasn't entirely my fault. They'd moved the Information Centre but failed to tell me. It now sits almost at the top of the hill rather than down at the bottom where my map suggested it was. Having spent several minutes wandering around, scratching my head and peering myopically into the building I thought should be the Information Centre–and probably at one time was–I made my way to the nearby supermarket where I bought a fresh pack of cigarettes and asked where they'd hidden the building I was looking for.

The last week or so's walking into Albany generally seems to be heralded as a high point. I didn't think so. I enjoyed the coastal paths but the closer I came to Albany the lower my spirits fell. When I should have been elated I was feeling down. There were probably a lot of reasons for this. The main one was the combination of the walk coming to an end and the return to reality. Having to face real life and all the questions and concerns it holds.

The last couple of days didn't appeal much at all. A lot of people, cars close to the path, walkways, stairs up and down to the beach, wind turbines and march flies.

Sometimes when you take a long walk you can become so absorbed in your immediate surroundings you actually forget which country you're in. Only your horizons really matter. The continent you're on becomes secondary to where you are right then, at that moment. This was driven home to me on the last morning when early on I arrived in a small and very busy carpark. On the path leading away from it stood rows of people, all looking out to sea. I squinted against the glare of the rising sun on water far below, couldn't see anything of excitement, decided to ask what all the fuss was about.

"Just checkin the surf mate. It's looking good this morning" was the reply.

Of course, how stupid of me, I was in Australia. What else would people be doing when looking out over the ocean early in the morning!

The hut at Sand Patch was brand spanking new, fresh out of the box. On checking the log book only one person had so far spent the night in it. I was going to stop there for breakfast/lunch but the march flies were such a plague I opted to continue and buy something hot and steaming and delicious when I reached Albany.

The trudge into town depressed me even more. Asphalt and concrete beneath my feet and filling my gaze. Cars, people, noise and hustle and bustle. Having bought my smokes and enjoyed one, having found out where the Information Centre now resided, I trudged up the hill and entered, went to the reception desk to fill in the final log book. This completed the girl at reception asked if I wanted to ring the bell.

The bell was donated by a couple who's son took his own life soon after completing a section of the track. The completion of the track is celebrated by the ringing of the hand bell, a way of honouring that life not completed. My heart went out to that couple, to the poor soul who had lost all hope. I rang the bell, realised just how lucky, how fortunate I was. My mood began to lift. I had bugger all to complain about.

As you will have gathered I've been a smoker–frequently a heavy smoker–all my life. I knew what my blood pressure was at the start of the walk and I knew what my body weight was. I'd promised myself that immediately I'd finished the walk I would go to a pharmacy and have blood pressure and weight checked, simply to see if the exercise, the limitations on diet, and the considerable reduction in smoking for a period of 8 weeks had made any difference. Unfortunately a biological imperative prevailed and when I went to ask the girl at reception for directions to the nearest pharmacy I found my brain had replaced the word 'pharmacy' with 'bakers'.

I followed the directions given, bought the biggest, fattest, pastie I could find and washed it down with a litre of iced coffee while sitting in the sunshine in the nearby park–sod the weight loss and blood pressure. I never did find out.

No sooner had I finished my healthy option lunch and lit a cigarette than LC phoned. She was elated to know I'd completed the walk, as elated as I should have been. We spoke for a long while and I was thrilled to hear her voice again after all those weeks. Finally my phone bleeped it was running low on battery. The phone call ended inconclusively. All I knew was that LC was happy to know I'd finished the walk successfully. No word of the future. In other words no future.

I have a mate in Albany. Pete is a good mate which is what mates should be. I'm lucky. I called and said I'd arrived. He told me just to make my way to his house. The dog was in the back yard so best I just stay out front. He'd be back by five.

I found where his house was on the map. I'd been there before but that was by car and I couldn't remember directions or location. It was a fair old walk from the centre but I had nothing else to do and having just walked one thousand kilometres I didn't think another few were likely to kill me.

Fortunately Chilli the dog remembered me, allowed access into the back yard where we communed in the shade of the porch until Pete returned from work.

That weekend was spent drinking beer, eating delicious fish washed down with equally delicious wine, talking and relaxing. It also involved getting up at silly o'clock in the dark of pre dawn to go fishing. Pete is your average western Australian bloke which means he fishes–a lot. My main memories are the relaxed conversation, the good wine, the good company, probably a feeling of satisfaction from having finished the walk. I pushed the future to the back of my mind for those two days. I'd cope with it later.

It did occur to me just to turn around and start walking back to Perth again, it's what I wanted to do most. Finances and approaching summer weather were against me, the risk of fire increasing with every step north. I abandoned this plan and on the Monday morning caught a coach north and back to Perth, my car, and an uncertain future. It was almost two months since I'd set out from that same city, head and heart a mess, no real direction or purpose in my life, the loss of LC gnawing at my heart like a cancer. And now I was returning, the only thing changed the season.

Consuming Passion?

Oh dear. I'm here–gear. Not my favourite topic but quite possibly one you've been waiting for? We are after all consumers and appear to be quite proficient, many of us accumulating so much and of such value that the situation upends. We no longer own it, it owns us–and often dictates what we do and how we live.

Again I'll take the opportunity to say I don't consider myself to be a conventional type when it comes to walking. I'm not really interested in gear. Most of the time I regard it as a necessary evil and try to make do with as little as I can so best you don't get yourself overexcited here. I do like wandering around outdoor shops and viewing all that's available, it's just that most of the time I can't really see the need for much of it–and can seldom afford it even if I did think it may be of benefit.

There is, for those who enjoy this aspect of walking, a complete gear list below. Probably best not take it as the ultimate in gear lists. It's not, it's simply what I took along, what made do. I'm not suggesting for a moment it's what you should take, that's up to you.

Let's do what I like to do best and keep things simple.

What's the most important aspect of any walk other than you yourself and your suitability to the walk you wish to undertake?

Yes, your feet, it's them what does the walking. Footwear is probably the single most important item you'll use, the one which will do most of the work.

Boots or shoes?–it doesn't matter so long as you are comfortable in them. I'm a boot person, always have been. Boots offer a bit of support, should prevent the ingress of foreign materials better than low cut shoes, give a bit of protection for ankles and reduce the chance of water getting in over the top. Loads of people wear incredibly light shoes these days and cover huge distances in them. These people have strong ankles, have to have. I'm told beach walking in soft sand is good for ankle strength and that sounds logical to me.

At the end of the day it doesn't matter what you choose to wear–clunky old fashioned leather boots, new lightweight boots, approach shoes or tatty old trainers ... so long as they are comfortable, fit you properly and won't cause problems. Footwear fit and comfort is much more important than manufacturers name, colour, fashion statement or cost. Buy what's right for you, not what you would wish to be right for you or what you fondly imagine looks right on you. How do you know what's right for you? You go to the best outdoor shop you know, get your feet measured, take professional advice, try on several different makes and models as suggested by the assistant attending you. Take all day over it if you like, don't rush. Footwear is a major investment and you will be wearing those boots or shoes or whatever a long time–if you get it right when you buy them.

Waterproof or not? Depends entirely on where you intend to do most of your walking, the conditions you anticipate. I don't like boots with allegedly waterproof linings. In my experience they make your feet hot and sweaty in warm conditions and few I've owned remained waterproof for long. Ask yourself–and possibly the sales assistant as well if required–a couple of questions. If you plan a long walk in the desert or some other low rainfall, generally dry and often hot area, do you anticipate wearing your waterproof jacket each and every day ... is it your every day attire? If not why not?

If you intend walking a lot in wet conditions then clearly footwear with a waterproof lining would be a sensible choice. Keep in mind this kind of footwear often takes longer to dry out than non-lined models.

Break your footwear in before ever committing time, effort and money to any major undertaking in them. Two or three days consecutive walking, with or without pack, should give good indication if you're going to suffer problems.

And now the truth. I ignored much of my own advice for the Bib. I was in the UK, had limited time to organise things, was too lazy. The boots I currently owned were gore-tex lined and already well past their sell by date, incapable of another 1000 kilometres without falling apart.

For years I've used Lowa lightweight desert boots in Africa and Australia. They fit my feet and I cannot rate them highly enough for use in hot, dry conditions. Unfortunately I couldn't obtain a new pair in the time allowed and my last long loved ones had been deposited in a bin in Exmouth the previous January. Last minute I bought a pair of Salomon Aero boots on the internet. Yes, I know! In my defence I have to say I had previously owned a pair of identical boots but with waterproof lining and knew they worked for me.

Lasting impressions? Excellent ... if they fit your feet. Probably the best ventilated boots I've ever worn. So well ventilated, so open is the weave of material, they allow dust and debris to pass through. Other than having very dirty feet this isn't a problem until you hit the beaches when they fill with sand and require regular emptying. I have no real complaints. Nothing is ever perfect. I completed the walk without a blister or hot spot, absolutely no problems with feet at all.

Socks can be just as important as boots/shoes. I have used medium or heavy weight wool socks for as long as I can remember, even in the desert. No problems, little smell.

A final word on footwear. A lot of the problems I've seen arise from boots being too small. You need at least an index fingers width between the ends of your toes and the front of the boots. Lowa recommend a boot size 15 mm longer than the actual length of your foot when you're standing on it. If necessary go up half a size–or more–to get that room. Wearing two pairs of socks is better than blisters, and wearing two pairs of socks won't mean the end of your walk.

What's the next most important item? I'd say your waterproof jacket if you anticipate wet weather. You get wet you get cold–you suffer, possibly even worse. There are a lot of seriously good options out there. Explain what you are using it for, take into account how much you might use it, take advice from experienced shop assistants. Many of them really do know what they are talking about. Sadly some of them don't.

I've tried all kinds of jackets over the years beginning way back with cotton ventile. Since then I've had gore-tex, simpatex, Patagonia storm. Few actually do what they say on the can–or should I say do it for very long. I settled years ago on the Patagonia version which makes you sweat like hell in humid conditions but is virtually bullet proof and does keep water out for year after year after year. A while back, on a trip to NZ, I bought a MacPac pertex jacket, light in weight and price. I love it. It probably won't last very long, especially if a pack is carried, but it does everything a waterproof breathable jacket should do and does it in spades. I'm kicking myself for never having tried Pertex before.

Your pack. Again take advice, have assistance while fitting, sift the bullshit out from the fact. Comfort comes first, weight second; pockets, accessibility, flash dangly bits and colour comes last. Capacity can be a bit of a bugger, cold conditions demanding more is carried in the way of clothing and food leaving you extra space in hot conditions, and we all know what we do with extra space–we fill it. On the Bib I used a 50 litre pack and it never appeared overloaded or stressed. Many I saw used larger packs, some used smaller.

Sleeping bag. Buy the best quality, lightest unit you can afford. Make sure it's warm enough, you'll be spending a lot of time in it and if you can't get warm you're not going to sleep and you're going to suffer fatigue. If it's too hot you can always unzip or just get out of it for a while, even just sleep beneath it if it opens up enough.

One thing worth mentioning about sleeping bags. They don't manufacture heat, they only store and reflect the heat produced by your body. Get into them cold and they will remain that way for quite some time. Get into them warm and they will warm up quickly. Don't expect miracles. The only heating element a sleeping bag has is you. Keep your sleeping bag dry in your pack.

Mattress. Again keep it light and go for something quality. The bigger it is the more comfortable it could prove to be–but it will also weigh and take space. Try and find a happy compromise. Take advice.

Stoves, pots, pans , etc. Jeez, we are spoilt for choice these days. Keep it light, keep it robust, keep it simple, keep it minimal, ensure you can obtain fuel for it. I've used the same MSR pocket rocket for 17 years and not yet had to change the 'O' ring on it.

All the rest of the clothing, etc. Again we are spoilt for choice. Merino works well and doesn't smell too bad even after days and days of use. Goose down is preferable to synthetic or fleece in bulk and weight but not in price. Choose a layering system, stick to it.

And that's about it in a nutshell. I told you not to become overexcited.

My personal kit list and additional details.

Pack. Osprey Exos 48 Excellent

Boots. Salomon X Ultra Mid 3 Aero Excellent

Rain gear. MacPac Pertex lightweight Excellent

(I didn't carry rain pants)

General everyday wear:

Cotton volly shorts courtesy of Target. Cheap, cheerful, comfortable

Icebreaker light weight merino wool t-shirt. Can't fault it

Smart wool hiker merino socks. Used these for years, very happy

Cotton bucket sun hat from Africa. It did the job

Cheap and cheerful sunnies, pharmacy specials.

Spares:

Cotton t-shirt courtesy of a wildlife conservation project in Namibia.

Cotton jeans.

Spare pair of Smart Wool socks.

Pair cotton boxer shorts (for when wearing jeans)

Teva sandals

Warmth:

Patagonia light weight zip necked fleece. 20 years old.

Patagonia zip neck puff ball pullover. 27 years old, full of holes.

Icebreaker merino beanie.

Buff.

Sleep:

Sea to Summit down sleeping bag.

Sea to Summit cotton/silk sleeping bag liner.

Sea to Summit light weight mattress. Began with a many times punctured 3 year old item which finally failed and refused to repair early on in the walk. The kind people at Paddy Pallin's in Perth send a replacement unit for collection in Donnelly River. Thank you PP staff, more than helpful, always good advice.

Pillow was the sleeping bag's stuff bag filled with clothing.

Cooking:

MSR pocket rocket. 17 years old.

Titanium 1L kettle with lid.

Sea to summit long handled spoon.

Plastic mug, no idea where it came from.

2x small zip lock bags, one for black pepper, one for mixed herbs.

General:

Swiss army knife. Large type with single locking blade and a few essentials like can opener, bottle opener, cork screw, plus a funny little spike on the upper side which I have no idea the use for–prizing boy scouts from girl guides?

1 x 1L Nalgene water bottle.

2 x 500mil juice bottles used for carrying water.

Reading glasses.

E-reader, charge lead and plug.

Cell phone and charge lead (same plug as used for E-reader).

A5 note pad and biro.

First Aid Kit. minimal

2 x Bic lighters.

Cigarettes.

Head torch. Petzl simple unit. Never required fresh batteries.

Pack of toilet paper.

Toothbrush and paste.

Disposable razor.

Cheap supermarket dish cloth used for washing and drying–both me and the cooking pot. Dried quickly.

4 metre length of thin cord for repairs or washing line.

Empty peanut butter plastic jar for holding cigarette butts.

I think that was it.

I used supermarket zip locks for electronics and note pad. Larger heavy duty zip locks held food and clothing respectively. They lasted the duration.

Sleeping bag lived inside a large Sea to Summit dry bag and never suffered even when it poured down and the inside of my pack was sodden.

Gas usage was about 3-4 days for 100 grams, max 10 days for 230 grams.

I never purified water. Occasionally boiled some if it appeared suspect but probably only did this a couple of times. Never had a problem. Only twice used more than 1L drinking water in a day but don't take that as advice for your own requirements. I tend to drink very little water for whatever reason. Best to drink a lot, more than you think you need initially. You can always pee.

Didn't start with walking poles but picked one up in Collie and carried it to the end.

Most used item? All of it was used regularly other than my rain jacket which saw only a few days action but was appreciated when I did need it.

Least used item? Again, everything carried saw use on a regular basis, nothing was superfluous.

Most appreciated luxury? My E-reader. Used on a daily basis, often for several hours. Never ran out of battery between rest halts when I could recharge it.

Heaviest item carried? LC, or the loss off, in my heart and in my head.

Weather:
Generally good, pleasant walking weather. Sometimes hotter than comfortable but never serious.
Six days of wet weather–not just occasional showers. Among these six days were two days of severe hail and lightning storms where I was lucky to find shelter off path, once in a hollow tree, the other time beneath a fallen log. After the second hail storm I found a dead parrot and a dead possum on the trail, evidence of the storm's severity in that particular place. These days were also the coldest and walking could be miserable ... but it's all part of the walk. Coldest section was around the town of Collie where night time temperatures dropped considerably. The coastal sections were cooled by sea breeze but never chilly.

Conclusion

That's it, the end of the walk, the end of the book. When I did finally reach Albany there was strong desire to turn around and start walking back north, to just keep walking. I have no real desire to continue the writing. I think I've said all I wanted to say, all that's worth saying. I hope you've enjoyed it.

But before I go, a few last thoughts about the walk and a few last snippets you may–or may not–find useful.

For any undertaking like the Bib allow yourself enough time, try not to set limits before you even begin. I met several people who were under constraints of time–had to be on a flight in three weeks–that kind of thing. They were putting themselves under pressure, unnecessary pressure, even before they'd begun. One of the pleasures of taking a long walk is removing yourself from the restrictions of time and obligation. Best make full use of it, enjoy it while you can.

This problem of pressure also applies to setting yourself goals. There is nothing wrong with goals, providing they are attainable. Persuading yourself you have to complete the walk in a set period of time because that's how long other's take, or a mate took, or you'll look a wuss if you don't ... that's just conforming to other's ideals and dictates. Walk your own walk, live your own life, let them live theirs. And besides, think how much you may miss by rushing through it all.

Would I do the walk again? In a heartbeat. Many people are fortunate enough to have done so already.

The Bibbulmun is not a wilderness walk. There are sadly few places remaining on Earth where the term can be used with any accuracy. For much of the early section the track runs close to major highways and traffic can be heard, especially at night when the air cools and sound travels well. Some others found this intrusive, the distant roar of a road train detracting from that sense of isolation, of being in the bush. Strangely enough I wasn't too bothered about it and can only attribute this to the fact I'd had a good look at the maps before setting out and recognised that in places the track came close to roads and a couple of the huts would be within earshot of passing traffic. I don't think I'd anticipated wilderness from the outset so had no great expectations. There are sections further south where the sense of isolation and remoteness is there. Savour them.

I don't think the Bibbulmun is a truly challenging walk, at least it wasn't in the way I chose to do it, making use of most of the huts and not rushing anywhere. You can make it a challenging walk if you wish, and many do. I reiterate, the Bibbulmun is a very user friendly walk, accessible and achievable for anyone of reasonable fitness and ability. The walker is highly catered too in respect of path, huts, water, restocks, advice and information.

I do think the Bibbulmun is a very enjoyable walk, which is why I'd do it again.

Would I do anything differently? Yes, probably. I'd take longer where possible, especially between Dwellingup and Northcliffe. I might take binoculars along ... perhaps even a bird book. I might also tarry a while longer in towns, trying to get a feel for them, absorb the ambience rather than just treating them as nothing more than a shower and restock point. They are after all part of the walk.

Would I change any of my kit? Nope. What I had worked well, did what it was designed to do, didn't break itself or my back or bank balance. I'd take exactly the same again. It all still works perfectly, why buy new?

Did I achieve my aim of 'walking it off' and shedding my skin like a snake, emerging new and fresh and reborn? No I didn't. I failed in this respect–though I may have learned something.

I've learned that though you may be able to flee pestilence and plague, war and famine, you cannot escape a broken heart because it dwells within you and goes with you everywhere you go. It's not distance or geography or hard physical exercise or even change of circumstance that prove the cure. Physical distance means nothing. Only distance in time can truly heal. I think my walk on the Bibbulmun Track was the fist step on that journey to recovery. Perhaps writing this book has been the second.

As a final piece of advice I offer this.

If you are to undertake the Bibbulmun track–or any other walk or adventure or time of new experience, revelation, excitement–don't do it alone. Unless you are a totally committed solo individual then take someone along with you. Take someone you love. Better still take someone who loves you in return. In this way your time on the track will not last a mere thirty days or sixty days. It will last a lifetime.

At the end of the day, in years to come when blisters have healed but back aches worse, all we are really left with is memories, and shared memories are richer.

In the words left scribbled by Chris McCandless, a young adventurer who's body was found in an abandoned bus in the wilderness of Alaska where he'd died alone ...

'Happiness only real when shared.'

Don't miss out!

Visit the website below and you can sign up to receive emails whenever Colin Valentine publishes a new book. There's no charge and no obligation.

https://books2read.com/r/B-A-XAPN-LKTMB

BOOKS2READ

Connecting independent readers to independent writers.

Also by Colin Valentine

Bibbulmun for the Broken-Hearted
Damaraland
African Essays

About the Author

Raised in rural Scotland Colin Valentine developed a keen interest in wild places and wild animals from a young age. These have been constants throughout his life and are now main themes in his writing. He's a firm believer that the only way to truly experience anywhere is by travelling slowly, on foot.

For the past two decades he's split most of his time between Australia where he's lived out of the back of a Subaru, and southern Africa where he lives out of a Land Rover. During these decades he's indulged his interests while attempting to give something back through commitment to wildlife conservation projects and working as a field guide.

He has no official home of his own, relying on the generosity of friends and family when he needs a roof over his head and somewhere to write.

Colin also believes we should be here for a good time as it's unlikely to be for a long time; and nobody should have to work for more than six months in any one year. He's made it a personal goal to prove this is possible. So far so good.